Distance Open Learning

Distance Open Learning
Challenges to Developing Countries

P. Renga Ramanujam

SHIPRA

Rs. 850

ISBN: 978-81-7541-522-5

2009 Edition
First Published in 2002

Distance Open Learning

Published by:

SHIPRA PUBLICATIONS
LG 18-19, Pankaj Central Market,
I.P. Ext., Patparganj, Delhi 110092, India
Cont.: 9650028065/47322068
Email: info@shiprapublication.com
Website: www.shiprapublication.com

Contents

Preface

In my previous book *Reflections on Distance Education for India,* I had discussed some of the issues related to distance education in India. I argued for greater degree of democratisation, quality and staff development in order for India to extend its educational activities to the masses who have either been carefully kept out of the mainstream education or given a second rate education in the name of 'second best'. While examining the above issues I could see a common pattern governing the practice of distance education in many of the developing countries which have similar or comparable issues, problems and challenges facing their educational systems and programmes, including the current practices and the future plans of distance education in their respective contexts.

'Distance Education' of the eighties is fast changing into Open Learning and nineties of the past century, at least in the advanced countries. The institutional concern in the previous decade and earlier had been to increase the access of education through distance mode supported by multimedia so as to make available some form of education to all those who needed it. Obviously, there were attempts to study a variety of learner profiles, their specific needs and learning styles with a view to designing, developing and delivering educational programmes which would suit the mostly independent study of distance learning. In this sense, distance education became 'learner centered', although the overall control and choice of curricula and courses rested with the distance teachers and the institutions of distance education. However, in the nineties, the emphasis shifted significantly from 'distance' mode to 'openness'.

'Open Learning' in the advanced parts of the world is increasingly becoming a real possibility because of the rapid changes continuously taking place in the field of communication technology. Computer technology and satellite communication have opened up a wide range of interactive media which enable the students of advanced countries to overcome the communicational barriers imposed by the physical distance between the learner and the teacher/institution in the context of distance education.

Because of the spread and growth of communication, globalisation of education is increasingly seen as a positive contribution of distance/open learning. Virtual universities and virtual classrooms have already started functioning through Internet, supern highways and satellite communication links. Television and Radio which broadcast political propaganda are now turning their attention to more and more clientele. CD-ROM and other computer devices like teletexts and teleprinting store volumes of information in compact disks, allowing students to choose what they want. 'Open Learning' in this context certainly makes room for students' freedom, although this freedom itself is open to debate on ideological grounds

Globalisation of distance and open learning is apparently encouraged and welcomed by the providers and receivers of education. The providers who have the necessary resources and marketing abilities sell their (educational) services in the free market, of course, for a price. Democratisation, quality education and cost effectiveness being the labels to attract the consumers, the 'buyers' or the 'receivers' of education too look for better quality products at cheaper rates. The learning institutions' efforts to fend for themselves on the self supportive plank in the advanced countries are too important to be ignored.

Leaving aside the socio-political implications of the self-supportive policies of educational institutions in the advanced countries for the learners in general and the distance learners in particular, one could at least dwell upon for a moment on their implications for the institutions in the developing countries. Developing countries going in for distance and open learning are faced with many compulsions and paradoxes. The compulsions are that they have to meet the educational needs of millions and billions of illiterate masses for the first time in their histories. They also have to find resources to do the impossible.

Since their resources are already restricted for the educational projects, they have to find ways and means to use the available limited resources. But the paradoxes are ingrained in their efforts to employ new, innovative strategies to achieve the educational goals in a short time without having the necessary experience and the infrastructure. On both the counts they have to depend on the institutions of the developed countries. Such a dependency, not surprisingly, makes the institutions of distance and open learning in the developing world fragile, and vulnerable to many risks and uncertainties.

If the developing countries have to develop appropriate strategies to achieve their educational-cum-developmental goals through distance and open learning, they should first develop appropriate models and the necessary human resources. Paradoxically, to evolve appropriate local models and expertise, the developing countries have to learn from the experiences of the developed countries. In the process, most often the developing countries tend to *adopt* or copy the success models, instead of *adapting* these. Because of this, it becomes extremely difficult for them to find right solutions to their problems.

The comparatively brief history of distance and open education in the developing world shows that the countries which have simply adopted the western models, especially the model of the Open University of UK, have run into difficulties. The local needs, learner characteristics, academic traditions, languages used as instructional media, access to technology, learning styles of distance learners and unfamiliar working environments of distance teaching institutions in the developing world do not really suit the adopted models to operate smoothly and effectively. Lack of appropriate flexibility and innovative approach to adapt the foreign models coupled with absence of local expertise also lead to wrong types of investment and wastage of resources. The institutions which have not followed a realistic approach to the practice of distance education in specific situations have succeeded only in creating huge edifices and much visibility through launching large number of programmes and courses, admitting large number of students and building certain infrastructure facilities without the necessary human resources to use them. Indonesia, and to a large extent India have followed the policy of adopting the British Open University model to establish their respective open universities at the national level. They have also gone for large scale expansion of their activities without allowing much time to monitor and evaluate their pilot programmes. The sudden expansion of large scale operations and adoption of a foreign success model have created numerous problems for both the institutions (UT, Indonesia and IGNOU, India) at the operational and implementational levels.

On the other hand, those developing countries which have chosen to evolve their own indigenous models or to adapt the foreign models to suit their local needs have shown notable evidences to prove the point that to stand on one's own strength is better than the dependent growth and protection. Venezuela and Costa Rica in Latin America, Zambia and Zimbabwe in Africa, and Thailand and China in Asia are some of the significant examples of countries, which have succeeded in developing their models or adapting other models appropriately to achieve their specific objectives.

There are obvious difficulties in choosing either of the two approaches : *adoption and adaptation*. In the first approach of adoption, everything looks bright and promising at the initial stages because of the local and external patronage to back up the institutions in the developing countries through funding, consultancy and equipment. However, in the long run, the adopted models find themselves in a situation where they seem to have everything but cannot use their resources because of their inability to build the internal mechanisms to function on their own. For every small issue or problem they look up to the external agencies to find the solution. Such a dependency suits the interests of the external success models but undermines the self-confidence of the staff working at the institutions of the developing countries.

In the case of countries which have indigenous models with inner strength, despite the initial reverses and setbacks, the institutions are in a position to resist the temptation of copying others and, therefore, to respond to the local needs, meaningfully and effectively. This inner strength of institutions is particularly important in the present context of globalisation. Globalisation, in simple terms means that those who have the resources and products of quality would expand their activities with least or no resistance from others throughout the world through mutual consent and agreements. In the context of distance and open education, this would mean the expansion of activities of institutions endowed with adequate material and human resources. Such an expansion takes place through the extension of their own academic programmes to others transcending the national barriers and also through aids and consultancy services. In the process, those institutions which have the wherewithall to meet their own needs and also the needs of others become the winners. And those institutions which do not stand on their own but continue to 'receive' from others become the loosers.

The increasing use of technology in distance education has a lot of promise and also poses some serious challenges in developing and delivering the educational programmes. While technology provides opportunities for the learners of the advanced countries to choose their ways to learn, in the developing countries it proposes to increase the educational access to the masses. In the latter case, the possibility of increasing the educational access through technology is intimately bound up with the access to technology itself. Granting that technology has potential to take education to the millions at greater speed, the questions related to availability, access and use of relevant technology for distance education need to be considered carefully, before institutions commit themselves to policies of technology and multimedia.

It may be comparatively easy for institutions to have access to sophisticated technology, but the same is not the case with students' access. Students' access to technology is still limited in the developing world and they have to depend more on the traditional means of interacting with their teachers and institutions. In the absence of adequate access to technology, the use of technology, even if it is available to institutions, will be on the periphery. Some of the distance education institutions like the Indira Gandhi National Open University, India have acquired very sophisticated technology for the purpose of greater interaction with students. But there are practical difficulties in achieving this goal because of the access question and the right kind of human resources to use the available technology. These are questions which defy simple answers.

The organisational structures of distance education institutions have definite influences on and implications for the work culture obtaining there. Though democratic culture is preferred to any other culture in educational institutions, it does not always operate in all distance education institutions. Depending on the socio-cultural environment and the institutional traditions, the staff-develop their working habits and attitudes towards institutional goals. Participation of staff in the decision making process at the institutions is basic to their involvement and sense of commitment in achieving those goals. Unless the organisational structures are democratic, one cannot expect the spirits of democracy to operate in the functional and operational areas of institutions. Autonomy, accountability and freedom of academic institutions do not acquire meaning, if these ideas are not given some concrete shape in the day-to-day functioning of the institutions. Distance and open learning institutions in the advanced world generally enjoy greater autonomy and academic freedom than their counterparts in the developing world. Partly due to historical reasons and partly due to the unequal sharing of global resources, the divide between the advanced world and the developing world continues to widen. This divide is being reflected in the educational standards, quality of staff and also the institutional cultures. The developing countries in general tend to adapt hierarchical models and bureaucratic culture in the establishment and management of institutions. Such a tendency is the result of the weakness in the socio-political traditions of these countries. Much of the conflict that arises in the working process is rooted in the organisational structures and management policies of the distance educators and the managements in many of the institutions aspiring to become democratic in the developing world.

Sharing of resources among distance education institutions both at the national and the international levels is becoming more of a necessity than a choice. Just as the economic argument is given as a justification for encouraging distance and open learning in place of conventional, face to face education, avoidance of duplication of efforts is given as the justification for sharing of available resources in distance education by the institutions concerned. Sharing is done through a variety of networking and collaborations. Europe, North America and Australia have shown a few models of networking to share their resources, expertise and experiences in open learning within and across the countries and continents. Globalisation in this respect is taking place very fast and it has entered the developing countries. Developing countries, on the other hand, have started thinking of 'sharing' only now. One reason for this time lag is their late beginning of distance and open learning itself. The other reasons pertain to their poor resources, expertise and experiences complemented by their inappropriate attitudes. But things are changing. The traditional notions about institutional autonomy and exclusive domains of teaching and research give way to institutional collaborations and mutual help. This change is also necessitated by the shrinking budget provisions made by the state for educational projects. Although the state's responsibility towards education of the citizenry is not given up anywhere, it is obvious from the funding from the state as they did in the previous decades. Naturally, those institutions which are not in a position to become competitive and self-supportive, have to accept the compulsion to share the available resources. If there are also valuable experiences to be shared, notions of autonomy and academic freedom need not acted as impediments to do so.

Some of the recent developments in the distance education scenario in he developing countries do hold some promises for making distance and open learning experience a truly rewarding one. However, these promises riddled with many loose ends have to travel quite a long and risky way before they could actually be realised. Indira Gandhi National Open University, India, for instance has the potential and fairly good infrastructural facilities, particularly in the electronic media, to emerge as a successful model for the developing countries with large populations and divergent cultures. But this potential is also delimited by some of the policies of the University in prioritising its programmes, appointing staff and orienting them to the new academic as well as work environment. The present challenge for the university is to shake off some of the ostrich like policies and look boldly towards future possibilities. Whether the challenge will be met in the way it should be, depends on many imponderables.

The issues listed above and many more of the kind are crucial to the success of distance and open learning in the developing world. I have tried to address some of them. The views I have expressed in this book would perhaps provide an occasion for colleagues in India and abroad to approach the issues raised here from different angles and with different perspectives. If this book could draw the attention of distance educators and persuade them to look at some of these issues critically, I shall be happy.

Acknowledgements

May I say that for the first time I see the need for acknowledging people collectively rather than mentioning their names individually? The major portions of my arguments in this book were inspired by the environment in which I work. Therefore, I must acknowledge the help I got from my colleagues and the policy makers at the Indira Gandhi National Open University—a help that cannot possibly be rendered by any single individual. By 'help' I mean only the kind of cultural and intellectual traits obtaining in one's work place which make or mar the academic excellence of distance and open learning projects. So much for the intellectual inducements that I derived to write this book.

At the more mundane level, I must acknowledge the help rendered by my wife Selvi who shouldered the domestic responsibilities stoically to allow me the 'intellectual freedom' to think and write with a morose face that invited not infrequently her sarcastic comments on intellectual activities in general. My elder son Sundar provided me the much needed comic interludes. Towards the end of writing this book my second son Sridhar arrived rather impatiently and defiantly as if to ask me whether I would complete this book at all! But I did complete writing it, though the discussion shall continue on the themes included in it. At the time of printing this book, Sridhar reads the "proof".

Dedicated to

my teacher, friend and critic

Professor S.V. Pradhan

1

Distance Education in the 21st Century: Implications for the Developing Countries

A Global View

The phenomenal growth of distance and open learning systems all over the world has drastically changed the educational scenario everywhere today. The conventional notions about teaching-learning are being replaced very fast by new ideas and strategies, thanks to the revolutionary changes continuously taking place in the media and communication. Since the concept of education as investment is also steadily gaining ground, even the poorest countries are slowly turning their attention to the educational needs of their respective populations in order to survive and develop. Distance education has been viewed by many as a viable strategy to achieve the national educational goals quickly and at low costs.

At present, there are 1300 distance and open learning institutions of different types and sizes located in 127 countries. The number of distance learners is approximately 100 million at the higher education level. It is expected to reach 120 million by 2025 A.D (Dhanarajan 1996). The available recorded data pertain mostly to institutions funded and/or recognised by the governments and the public bodies. If we add to these the private and unregistered institutions and the students learning through them, the figures will be still higher. In India, about 25 per cent enrolment at the higher education level is with distance teaching institutions.

In India alone as per the latest data available in 2001 there, were about 70 distance teaching units called Correspondence/ Distance Education Departments located within conventional universities, 9 State Open Universities and 1 National Open University (AIU Handbook 2001). Over 1000,000 students we are on the rolls of these institutions in 1999. At the school level, the National Open School offers education to about 500,000 students spread across the country. Besides these, distance teaching porgrammes are offered by some private institutions and television companies (*e.g.* ZED programmes by Zee TV, the management programmes offered by Jain TV, Sun TV and others). Roughly about 25% of the student population at the higher education level is already taken care of by the correspondence/ distance/open learning systems.

The expansion of the distance and open learning system in other countries—both developed and developing—has established beyond any doubt the fact that this system is going to play a very important role in the 21st century. The present dominance of campus based higher education may become a thing of the past perhaps by the middle of the next century, if not earlier. Possibly the merger of the two systems may take place faster than expected, and it may lead to new structures of educational institutions and the strategies which may be used by both campus based and distance mode institutions. If that is the trend, then, what will be the implications of it for the developing countries?

The implications could be many but most important of them will be for the economy, sovereignty and culture of the people of the developing world. How the growth of distance and open learning will impact the areas seemingly unrelated to education in the developing nations can be accounted for by analysing the nature of demands made by the system on the resources of a country, the curriculum, methodology and the managerial process as a whole. Besides these, the cost factor which is usually assumed to be cheaper in the distance education system plays a major role in promoting the system in place of face to face campus based education.

Distance Education in the Developed World

Distance education scenario in the developed world presents a comparatively bright and promising picture for the 21st century. The Open University, UK, for example, has become the country's largest university which now plays a central role in the credit transfer and award validation mechanisms that knit British higher education and training together (John Daniel, 1995). In general, the European Distance Education Network (EDEN) shows that the European countries have firmly recognised the Distance and Open Learning system as part of their educational enterprise. North America, Australia and Japan have developed their own distance teaching—learning systems in many forms flexible enough to cater to the varied needs of their different learner clientele (Sewart 1995). Advancement in communication devices which are widely used by the distance and open learning institutions in the developed countries make it possible the individualised teaching-learning there. Besides, the well established academic traditions and a wider provision for basic primary and secondary education have created a strong base for extending higher, vocational and unconventional educational programmes to those segments of adult populations who have limited or no access to campus based face-to-face education in the different areas at the tertiary level.

A brief overview of the prominent features of distance and open learning scenario in some of the advanced countries would give us a better understanding of the situation in those countries. For example, in the United Kingdom, Germany, France, Norway, Sweden, Spain, the United States of America, Canada, Japan and Australia the distance/open learning systems operate very effectively for the following reasons:

- Adult learners with an appreciable degree of basic/primary/ secondary education.
- Medium of instruction that is mostly the mother tongue of the learner.
- Availability and accessibilty of well-equipped, advanced technology and communication facilities.
- Institutions with clear vision and mission statements.
- Adequate resource mobilization.

- Thoughtful and committed academic leadership.
- Flexible and need based curriculum.
- Committed and/or trained, qualified staff.
- Thorough planning and implementation of educational programmes.
- Adequate and efficient student support services
- Continuous and systematic monitoring, review and evaluation.
- Political will (which is crucial) to back up the projects and institutions.

Historically, the advanced countries in the West and also Japan had developed a very good network of communication systems. In the 19th century, locomotives, road transport, steam navigation, telegraphs and telephones speeded up the process of transportation and communication in Europe. The industrial revolution made it necessary for nations to invent new means of communication and transport to carry out their economic, trading, commercial and military activities successfully. As a byproduct of these, experiments with new ways of teaching-learning started, though slowly and on a limited scale. Humanistic education was still struggling against the centuries old sectarian-religious dogmas in the 19th century when the campus based classroom teaching was emerging as the dominant mode. Isaac Pitman, in a way planted the seed of the modern correspondence education when he started offering postal tuition on short-hand in 1840 in Britian. Pitman would not have imagined that after a century his small educational venture would grow into a significant mode of education spread in many forms in the United States of America, Australia, Western Europe and Canada in the late nineteenth and early twentieth centuries. Since campus based, classroom teaching was confined to the upper classes and the middle classes in the industrialised nations, the forceful demand for education from the working classes and other deprived sections of the society had to be met through some means. After the second world war, the demand was felt all the more urgently because the issue had a potential to disturb, if not overthrow the existing social order, and the ruling classes could ill afford such an eventuality that would lead to social unrest.

The concept of the 'welfare state' was gaining importance, presumbaly with the approval of the ruling classes, through out western Europe in order to contain the spread of social revolutions which had already covered one third of the globe in the late 1940s. As a part of the welfare state concept, new ways of meeting the increasing educational demands of the people were also to be sought. At the higher educational level, the open university system became the flagship to meet the challenge.

The history of the establishment of the Open University in the United Kingdom in1969 makes it abundantly clear that the labour government's policy to expand higher education through the Open University was the least 'revolutionary' in the classical sense of the phrase. Nevertheless the project had to be pushed through with skill and determination because of the perceived social threat in it by the conservatives (Perry 1976). It is a different matter that later on the Thatcherite conservatives too found it useful to ward off dangers from the lower classes demanding more of their share in the educational domain. The Open University is an example of how a harmless palliative can be projected as a revolutionary measure by the left of the centre politicians which in turn would be perceived as a threat and therefore opposed by the die hard conservatives. Neither of the stances did substantially alter the role of open universities and distance education, as is evidenced by the experience of many countries in the advanced world.

Distance Education in the Developing World: The Historical Backdrop

However, the effectiveness of distance education institutions is contingent upon many factors. In the developing world, every small measure to expand education at any level is hailed as 'radical' by the governments themselves. But many of the proclaimed 'radical' programmes had failed in the past mainly because of:

1. lack of clarity in policy formulation and setting of institutional goals,
2. inadequate material support and political will, and
3. lack of human resources.

Modernisation being the overall aim of educational systems of the developing countries, the states have greater responsibility in allocating resources and expanding education at all levels. However, the state intervention in educational matters has its own dangers. Instead of developing the democratic values and liberating attitudes in citizens, the state funding may very well demand subservient behavior from the educated. In the context of adult education for example, W.E. Styler (1984) observes:

> *The developing societies have provided a number of instances which adult education schemes have been interfered with, even abolished, because they represent political attitudes, particularly in favour of freedom of thought and expression which appear dangerous to the regime in power.*

The Spread of knowledge through education has always been a threat to the establishment or the existing social order. In the classical period of capitalist expansion—what is euphemistically called the industrial revolution—liberal and secular education had to fight its way to come out of the sectarian clutches of the church which held the ideological sway over the minds of the people under feudalism that existed for centuries. Liberal and secular education was necessary for the new industrial-technological society to grow and expand. New ideas in the field of politics sprang up to consolidate the gains of democracy. Scientific temper and intellectual adventure became the hallmarks of education and relative intellectual tolerance became the backbone of liberal democratic society.

However, the enlightment of liberal democracy, even in the best of civilized nations did not extend beyond the ruling classes, so far as the sharing of the fruits of the new industrial civilisation was concerned. The working class, at the best, has to remain in the periphery of liberal education, and the diluted, philanthropic educational alms doled out to them through the sunday schools by the 'kind hearted' religious missionaries. Basic literacy prepared them to operate the machines in the factories and read the Bible in the church on Sundays. Literacy, thus, enabled the workers to become skilled labourers without whom the wheels would not run. It also persuaded them to imbibe the

Biblical, spiritual sedatives without which their souls would not calm down. Till the working class leaders came up with their own agenda of 'workers' education, liberal education practically remained education of the ruling middle classes of Europe. When the industrialised nations became colonisers, the educational system in the colonies too underwent traumatic experiences. The old belief system along with the educational one caved in. Without much resistance, the colonised became the willing recipients of English education, for example in the name of modern education, at the cost of their native academic traditions and languages. If Macaulay's statement on the need for English education in India can be taken as the essential objective of colonial curricula, then, the consequence of English education in India are generalisable in their essential aspects to all the British colonies, though the details may vary here and there. Thomas Macaulay said:

> *Anglicist educational policies reflected the power and self-confidence of Britain and were designed to create a class who would be interpreters between us and the millions whom we govern, a class of persons Indian in blood and colour, but English in tastes, in opinions, in morals and in intellect, who would be consumers of British goods, provide recruits for the subordinate ranks of the East-India company's civil service and be loyal to the Raj (Basu 1991).*

By and large, the colonial system of education did serve the purpose anticipated by Macaualy and other colonial ideologues and administrators. But the unintended results also did come out. English education in India, for example, sowed the seeds of democracy and national liberation which in due course grew into a large network of English educated intellectuals who spearheaded the national liberation movement. The Indian experience has been similar to the experiences of other colonised countries. What is true of the British colonialism is also true of the French, Dutch and other varieties

The post-Second World War world has witnessed many social and political changes. National liberation movements till the late 1960s, the communist revolutions in China, Mangolia,

Vietnam and Eastern Europe, and the cold war between the two super powers — the USA and the former USSR—dominated the agenda of all political, economic and intellectual gatherings untill the mid 1980s. In the early 1990s the upheavals in the East European countries, the subsequent collapse of the Soviet Union, the two Gulf wars and the economic globalisation of the unipolar world have had far reaching impact on the national agendas of developing countries. The NATO bombing of Yugoslavia shows that no country can now assume that it is safe in any part of the globe. The terrorist attacks in New York and Washington on 11 September 2001 have exposed the fragility of the modern civilisation as a whole.

After becoming politically independent, most developing countries have been caught up in the complex struggle of nation building and modernisation. Since they did not have strong economic and educational bases to cope with the challenges, they had to inevitably depend on the developed western countries, most often their erstwhile colonial masters to get the expertise and assistance to create their own indigenous resource bases. This dependence has been one of the historical tragedies which very few developing countries have been able to avoid. Both nation building and modernisation need economic and human resources. One of the devastating results of colonialism has been the depletion of indigenous institutions of all kinds—economic, political, cultural and intellectual. These institutions, of course, were pre-modern and dominated by feudal ideologies of different types. During the colonial period they had been systematically destroyed by the policies adopted by the colonial rulers inorder to perpetuate their own rule and, thus, their interests.

The intellectual domination of the ruling classes, be they native or alien, does play an alienating role at all levels. The native ruling class would not allow the common masses to have the best available education. The alien ruling classes would allow the native elite to have the second best education only, so as to make the intelligentsia of the colonised country dependent on or subservient to the rulers. It also happened that some sections of the colonised populations at the lowest strata were given some kind of western education that converted the natives into loyal servants of the rulers. In the process, colonial system of education had effectively destroyed the native academic and intellectual traditions and in their place transplanted fragile and anemic institutions which would neither compare well with those of the ruling nations, nor can grow in the native soil to meet the demands and needs of the local populace. In India, for example, English education became the status symbol of the elite. The Maharajas, the landlords and the Brahmins were the first to take to English education and the European customs and Etiquette. Although English education did make it possible for a few nationalist leaders to emerge, on the whole, it had a destructive effect on the educational institutions and intellectual traditions of the colonised people in general

On the other side, the Christian missionaries spread English education along with the religion by reaching the most socially backward and humiliated members of the lower castes and converted them to Christianity by giving them English education, the Bible, and the much needed human dignity. It so happened that the educated members of the lower castes eventually got better status than the so-called upper castes in India. The aggregated result was that the educated section of the country was totally alienated from the vast majority of the people. Since the native languages and the native academic institutions as well as traditions were not considered modern enough to secure the government jobs, positions, power and status, they remained neglected much too long. By the time the colonised countries became politically free, the 'civilised' world had travelled very far in education, technology and other fields of human development. But the independent developing countries had to begin their nation building and modernisation somewhere. And they began by imitating the western models.

The Current Educational Challenges before the Developing World

Economic development in the developing countries largely depends on the western technology. Educational polices and practices, therefore, get moulded to meet the demands made by the western technology on the developing world as a whole. The campus based instruction in the newly independent countries of Asia and Africa needed more material and human resources but the governments could not spare much for educational budgets. In most developing countries the defence budgets are disproportionately higher than their economic growth and educational attainments.

Although the aim of the developing countries has been to build their economies by way of modernising their education, their policies and practices usually run into rough weather, mainly because of limited resources, poor grasp of the policies needed and the inadequate human resources. On the one hand, they stand on a weak economic and technological base, which does not permit faster indigenous growth of knowledge, industry and technology. On the other hand, they become further dependent on the developed countries when they borrow liberally from left and right to meet their defence requirements which are usually manipulated than real. As they become the dumping grounds for the outdated weapons as well as technology of the advanced countries, there has been little evidence to show that the developing countries can ever become modern and economically strong in the same way as the advanced countries are. The invisible exploitation of the poorer countries by the rich has its impact on the technologies and educational development of the former. Often artificial data are cooked up to show that the developing world has made tremendous progress in every sphere. Actually, the donor countries stand to gain at the cost of the recipients. This general rule does not get disproved by the exceptions like South Korea, although the success of the South Korea cannot be taken as a typical case of other developing countries.

Even today, 50 years after the establishment of the United Nations Organisation with the aim to achieve global equality, peace and human rights, 80 per cent of the global resources are used by 20 percent of the world population which lives in the developed world. The unequal sharing of resources gets reflected in the standards of living, economic stability, educational facilities, health and other aspects of nations. Obviously, the educational standards of the poorer countries remain low. Any suggestions that introduction of distance education in itself can raise the standards of education or solve the educational problems of the developing countries are fallacious, misleading and self-defeating. Without a strong resource base, which includes money, human resources and infrastructural facilities, trial and error methods of implementing distance education projects will further worsen the situation. Often, political statements are being made about he expansion of distance education systems in the developing countries only in terms of number of institutions, courses and student enrolment. The latest information made available in CD-ROM by ICDL shows 107 countries having 1117 distance teaching institutions offering 38,694 courses to 50 million students (ICDL Database 1999).

But there is hardly any information readily available on the number of students who have completed their courses or how the programmes have contributed to the individual development or to the economic and technological aspects of nation building. Nor are many studies available on the cultural impact of new technologies on the poor countries (Miller, 1995).

The term used in the literature of distance and open education such as 'adult learner', 'independent study', 'learner autonomy', 'mediated two-way communication', 'multimedia', 'multi-channel learning', 'open learning', 'life long learning', 'experiential learning' etc. extrude western cultural connotations and they are too general to take care of the specific socio-cultural variations of the people living in the developing world.

An analysis of the socio-cultural contexts in which the above terms were originally coined and used would show that the advanced western countries conceived distance education concepts on the basis of their technological growth, cultural heritage and academic traditions. Not that there are no conflicts among the educational philosophies of western countries with regard to distance education. The on going debates in the developed world on the sociological and pedagogic implications of technology based teaching-learning, the philosophical principles which shape the distance learning curricula, the ideological biases incourse contents, the cost factor, marketability of educational enterprises and other issues have much relevance to distance education in the developing world. However, the level of the debates as such shows that the concerns of distance educators in the developing countries are more at the basic level. The concerns are such as the following :

1. Can some sort of education reach the people?
2. Can the shrinking educational budgets meet the minimum infrastructural requirements?
3. Will there be an appreciable degree of success in the course completion rates?
4. Are there job opportunities for those who complete their studies through distance mode?
5. Are there enough arrangements to provide education to those who want it, irrespective of its use value?

These and similar issues dominate the thinking of the policy makers and administrators in the developing countries.

Surveying the distance education scenario in a number of developing countries in Asia, Africa and Latin America, Manjulika and Reddy (1996) observe the following common features:

- Inadequate finances
- Poor communicational and infrastructural facilities
- Absence of clear governmental policies
- Limited use of audio-visual media
- Shortage of experts to develop multimedia courses
- Lack of financial and academic autonomy for distance-teaching institutions
- Low social and academic status of distance education because of quality issues.

Individual studies on the specific problems of developing countries have been studied by a number of researchers (See Arger 1990; Holmberg 1989, Peter Smith *et al* 1987).

However, the conclusions and generalisations which are to be derived from the specific contexts are very significant for this discussion. What appears to be quite obvious from the point of view of academic research becomes important when looked at from the political, cultural and sociological angles of the current distance education scenario.

Some research studies have posed the questions related to distance educator in the developing countries frankly and directly (Arger 1993; Villoroel 1995; Oliveira and Rumble 1991). Others have given descriptive analyses of the needs, issues, possibilities, challenges, etc. of the developing countries practicing distance education. But the descriptive details in themselves are significant. The overall aims of distance education curricula, the characteristic features of the student clientele, the infrastructural facilities such as buildings, electricity, postal services, transport, telecommunications, the television–radio network etc. and the human resources to use the facilities, especially the media technology when made available, are the key factors which must engage the attention of distance educators in the developing world. These factors have utmost significance in the context of proposing distance education as the viable alternative strategy to tackle the educational problems at the national level in many developing countries. But what does actually happen in the developing world?

The Open University and the Developing World

The success of the British Open University in the seventies obviously acted as the inspiration for policy makers in many developing countries to establish their own open universities or distance teaching units. In India, for example, the thinking of establishing an open university at the national level had been there for a decade before it actually materialised in 1985 with the establishment of Indira Gandhi National Open University (IGNOU) (Parthasarthy Committee Report 1974). Although the Andhra Pradesh Open University (now Dr. B.R. Ambedkar Open University) was established in 1982, the blueprint prepared for a full fledged open university was given some kind of practical shape only in the establishment of IGNOU which is broadly modeled after the Open University, UK. In 1974, *i.e.*, five years after the OUUK came into existence, Pakistan established the Allama Iqbal Open University (AIOU) at Islamabad. The AIOU has been guided by consultants from the UK from its inception.

Thailand established its two major open universities Sukhothai Thammathirat Open University (STOU) and

Ramkamhaeng University (RU) in 1978 and 1971 respectively. Although Thailand too got the inspiration from the success story of the OUUK, it has deviated a lot in adapting the Open University system to suit its local needs. SriLanka (1981) Bangladesh (1988) Malaysia (1980) Hongknog (1990) Singapore (1991) and South Korea (1983) are some of the other important examples of countries having drawn inspiration from the British Open University.

However, the British Open University itself was the result of Herald Wilson's inspiration that he got from the former USSR when he visited it in 1956 and saw the tremendous success of distance education of a different sort which was centrally planned and implemented by the Soviet State to meet the educational demands of the country. The East European countries, the former German Democratic Republic, Cuba, Nicaragua, Zimbabwe and Tanzania are other notable examples which have modelled their educational policies and practices on the basis of the experience of the USSR. In the post-Mao Peoples' Republic of China distance education got an impetus through radio and television broadcasting. Central Radio and Television University (1978) CRTVU is one of the biggest institutions in the world which provide education to workers who need to update their technical and vocational skills.

Distinction or the Divide?

What really distinguishes the distance education of the developed countries from that of the developing world is the over all aim set for it. In the developed countries the broad aim is to provide education to individuals who need it at different levels with different individuals needs. In the developing countries the aim becomes a collective one such as nation building, eradication of illiteracy, rural development, health education, women's education, tribal education, education of the socially disadvantaged etc., besides the usual academic, technical and vocational programmes. The very magnitude of the aims/goals set before distance education in the developing countries makes the educational operations very complex and demanding. The potential of distance education is stretched too far to meet every educational need which has not been met so far. This has put tremendous pressure on the systems of distance education, which are yet to take firm roots.

In one way, distance education is perceived as the solution for all the shortcomings of conventional, face-to-face education in the developing countries. In another way, it is projected as the cost effective, and therefore a cheap way of meeting the demands of education. In the process, too little money is allocated to meet too many educational needs. As a matter of fact, much of the educational crises in the developing world can be traced to the same economic arguments. Because the educational budgets in these countries have been usually small, the standard and the quality of education too have not been high. The spread of literacy and the expansion of education at different levels have suffered precisely because of the meagre allocation made to all the educational projects. This fact is usually ignored by those who criticise the face-to-face education and attribute every educational fiasco to it. If the funding of education is rationalised on a scientific basis, perhaps distance education could meet the demands much faster and more efficiently than the lumberous, rigid and expensive structures of campus based education. Inspite of all the possible hurdles, distance education has been spreading rapidly. There is no reason to believe that the hurdles cannot be overcome. What is really needed is a systematic appraisal of the impact of distance education in the developing countries over the decades to find out the strength and the weaknesses for the systems as obtaining in many countries. The weaknesses, once identified would persuade the practitioners to go for remedial measures. If remedial measures are not taken consciously with sufficient political will, then, there is every possibility of turning the system into a self-serving agent which may serve the interest of a few individuals but the system as such will not achieve the intended goals of nations and peoples.

Lack of Resources: African Scenario

Paucity of material and human resources has in general affected the practice of distance education in every developing country that has not been able to achieve its educational goals. Here I will present a typical case. Ethiopia started its distance education project in the early 1960s. But it did not have either the necessary infrastructural facilities nor the expertise in designing, developing and implementing its educational programme.

During 1962-64 the Distance Education Division (DED) invited an American Dean of the Extension Division of Nebraska University as a consultant to help design the course to serve the needs of Ethiopia. The American, while doing the 'needful' for Ethiopians, actually imported the secondary level courses from Nebraska, the USA. As one could expect, the courses did not meet the requirements of the students of Ethiopia. After evaluating this unrewarding excerise, the American Dean, and local experts tried to develop courses which would suit the local needs. However, after exploring the 'possibilities' of developing the local need based courses, the attempt, along with the idea was given up because of "lack of resources and expertise in distance education". (Inquai, S. 1992)

Although two staff members of DED had been sent to the National Extension College (NEC) and the International Extension College (IEC) London, to get the necessary training to develop the relevant courses in Ethiopia, on their return the staff members did not make use of their training of whatever kind, because the university which arranged for their training did not encourage them. As a result Ethiopia has not been able to make any headway in establishing a distance education system, nor had it succeeded in creating a good department of distance education either. The Distance Education Division (DED) of Ethiopia is presently "passing through a period of doldrums which seems to be the result of long neglect, under-financing, and under-staffing", besides suffering from lack of good leadership (Inquay, S. 1992)

Ethiopia is an extreme example, but the features of he Ethiopian case are generalisable to describe the situation in many a developing country which does not have the necessary resources and a reasonable degree of expertise.

Kenya, one of the richest countries in Africa, has not been able to articulate its educational needs with a future perspective. As a result, it had not made available sufficient funds and human resources to create a relevant, indigenous model of its own to serve the needs of Kenyan students who otherwise cannot have access to face-to-face education. In the absence of strong governmental efforts to meet the demands in this area, private and foreign agencies readily step in to take advantage of the opportunities. And that is what exactly has happened in Kenya too.

For many years, private, mainly British correspondence colleges have offered distance education courses to health workers and school teachers in Kenya (Holmberg, 1990). When efforts were made by the state, distance education in Kenya looked up to the future, although a number of factors related to resource mobilisation hamper the development of the system at the national level. Limited electricity supply, poor postal services, expensive equipments used by untrained staff in non-professional way and a large body of untrained teachers create problems for a healthy and faster development of the system. Although competent academics are available in Kenya, their number appears to be comparatively small and the distribution of this small number of competent people across the distance teaching units may not lead to effective utilisation of their talents because of the generally unprofessional environment which, of course, is not a unique privilege of Kenya alone. Added to these, is the problem of language as a medium of instruction. Although English is one of the two official languages of Kenya playing a dominant role in administration, education, journalism and business, the mastery of English by a majority of Kenyan teachers is regrettably low. Poor mastery of English which is the medium of instruction, slow administrative process and lack of resources inevitably slow down the speed of distance education in Kenya—a country, rich in its oil and natural resources, unlike Ethiopia.

Zambia has made tremendous advancement in distance education in recent years. However, inadeaquate material and human resources negatively affect the quality of the programmes as well as the learning process. While acknowledging the achievements of distance education in

Zambia, Mulenga (1987) identified "some difficulties, particularly in course development and student services which reduce the quality of the distance education offering ". Zambia, though a small country as compared to Kenya, Ethiopia and India can however, boast of greater success in its endeavor to promote distance education because of its rational resource allocation, concern for quality and care for setting achievable goals and proper planning. In general, distance education in African countries suffers from the same malnutrition that impoverishes educational institutions in other developing countries: shortage of resources.

Analysing the trends in teacher education in the third world Gary Coldwin and Som Naidu (1989) identify population growth and the shrinking resources for primary education as two of the other important reasons for the poor quality of education, including non-availability of trained teachers—"particularly in the rural areas where the majority of people reside" which make the practical operations difficult and complex. The perennial contradiction in implementing the educational programmes in the developing countries, thus, is that of greater needs of education at every level and the grossly inadequate resources to meet them.

Latin America

Latin America had been struggling at least for two decades till the mid eighties to come to grips with its own problems with respect to deciding on the suitable models of distance education. Rumble (1985) observed the peculiarities of the Latin American situation in the early eighties and noticed doubts being raised by the Latin American educators about the suitability of the Biritish Open University model in the severely under funded, poverty stricken and illiterate nations usually governed by authoritarian regimes. The most significant problems adversely affecting the Latin American distance education have been: shortage of resources to create infrastructural facilities, shortage of trained educational managers to plan and operate a distance education system, and the highly politicised nature of university structures which make innovative educational projects very fragile.

Although doubts were expressed about the future of distance education even in the eighties, the concept has taken firm roots and in certain respects it has contributed significantly as a model for the developing world which we shall discuss later.

Theses on Distance Education for the Developing World

After having considered some significant experiences of the practice of distance education in the developing world, one could advance the following theses, which may draw the attention of distance educators:

1. There are greater perils and dangers involved in blindly copying any western models of distance education than in evolving indigenous models for the developing countries even if the latter meant absence of theory and experience.
2. Indigenous models, though very difficult to evolve quickly, once created will have greater relevance and strength than the copied or adopted models.
3. It is possible to create a variety of models which will be equally effective in different specific social-economic and cultural contexts irrespective of success models recommended by the 'experienced' distance educators.
4. The future of distance education in the developing countries would depend more on the ability of distance teaching institutions to respond to the specific needs of learners at different levels and less on their resourcefulness to catch up with their counterparts in the developed world.

Let me substantiate the above with some evidence.

Asian Experience

Indonesia offers another classic example of a developing country which got inspiration from the successful western models of distance education but in the practice of distance education got trapped, because of blind adoption of success models. Indonesia has its strong traditions of teaching-learning which resemble any other Asiatic academic tradition of respecting the teacher and expecting from him knowledge and wisdom to flow. Besides this reverential treatment of teachers and teaching, the low literacy rate and strong oral traditions do not adequately prepare the teachers as well as the learners to benefit from distance education as practised in the west.

The first obvious mistake that every developing country including Indonesia makes, is to ignore the ground reality where too many incomparable variables distract the smooth functioning of a model which might have been a success in a developed country. In the context of distance education, the concept and strategies of self-learning have to be applied cautiously and imaginatively. Without the psychological and cultural preparedness of both the teachers and the learners, distance teaching and self-learning will not be successful. The necessary preparedness does not come to them without changing their social, economic and cultural orientation to the extent necessary to receive the concept and adapt it to suit their own conditions. Raden Dunbar (1991) while addressing some of the above mentioned issues in Indonesia observes that the "fundamental cause of distance education failure in Indonesia has been the *adoption* of western models, without *adaptation* to suit the acculturised behaviours of Indonesian teachers and learners".

Indonesia, has a large population, strong Islamic culture, oral traditions of teaching which hold the teachers with high respect and view learners as 'receivers' of knowledge. It has high population growth rate, low literacy rate, limited access to sophisticated technology and a fragile democratic polity. Obviously, it cannot be expected to succeed in practising distance education in the way it is done in Europe or North America. Nor can it increase its educational budget to the extent necessary to provide resources for face-to-face education to meet the educational needs of the people entirely. The possible alternative would be the creative adaptation of some successful model of distance education. But Indonesia went for *adoption* rather than *adaptation* when it established its Open University in 1984—the Universities Terbuka (UT).

> *The obvious choice of a model for UT was the UK Open University. Naturally the UTs strategies to impart distance education were based on the strategies of UKOU. UT started its activities with a big bang, admitting*

60,000 students for its courses in 1984. And in 1990 about 270,000 students enrolled for the various courses of UT. But the success rate of course completion was anything but satisfactory. The University was beset with all kinds of problems and difficulties in carrying out its plan, particularly in the crucial areas of course development and course delivery. The reasons for the unrewarding exercise are not far to seek. (Dunbar, 1991).

Any developing country going in for adopting a foreign, especially a western success model is bound to find itself in a tricky, difficult situation, if it fails to adapt the model to suit its own specific situation and plan its activities with a strong sense of realism. Because of uncritical enthusiasm, the planners of distance education in the developing world want to do things in their respective countries in the way the western institutions have done and succeeded, forgetting the latter's specific concerns, resources, experience and traditions. This uncritical enthusiasm of the planners of the developing world may have three sources: (I) a genuine lack of understanding about the implications of adopting western models, (ii) a desire to please the political bosses by doing something visible for political and publicity purposes and/or (iii) the vested interests of some key players to do things which would suit their personal interest rather than the interests of the institution and the learners. One or all the above can be seen operating behind the planning and execution of distance education projects in the developing countries. Indonesia too must have had its share of this sad experience.

The planners of UT indeed, heavily depended on the western models and the western consultants from the UK, Cananda and America. UT's experience in adopting the UKOU strategies in course development and course delivery, though sadly disappointing, has a few valuable lessons to offer to the developing countries which would like to start their own distance teaching. Commenting on the failure of the strategies adopted by the UT for its course development and delivery Dunbar (1991) says:

The assumption appears to have been that Indonesian distance teachers and learners would behave in much the same way as their western counterparts when faced with teaching and learning via mediation, most eventually mastering the technique of education without a direct and continuous personal relationship with a teacher.

The assumption was obviously proved wrong, because of the fundamental variation in culture of teaching-learning between the country which created the model and the country which adopted it. Besides the cultural implications, one could easily discern the other possible reasons: variations in the infrastructural facility, access to technology and provision for a strong student support service. A team of evaluators from UNESCO – ICDE studied the myriad problems faced by the UT in 1990. Summarising the situation at the UT the report by the UNESCO – ICDE team says:

UT would appear to be beset by a daunting number of problems of a fundamental nature that will require some dramatic, if not traumatic, changes to be made before it can be accepted by the community as a viable alternative to traditional forms of education. The educational philosophy and the current organisational arrangements that have been designed to support it are clearly not working.

Similar discoveries will be made sooner or later about the non-working models and strategies adopted by many other developing countries, including India. I analyse the IGNOU experience in a separate chapter which would show the similarities between UT and IGNOU in some crucial respects. The most important lesson from both these and similar experiences for the developing world is that the blind copying of any successful western model of distance education would not work in the developing world but, what is much more alarming, it would discredit the very philosophy of distance education in the situations dominated by traditional notions of education, and thus hamper its growth for a long time to come.

Strengths of Indigenous Models

As a refreshing contrast to the experience of Indonesia and some other developing countries, the Latin American experience is one of self-confidence and independent thinking. Although many Latin American experiments with distance education had to meet with disappointing experiences and even failures, the grim determination with which some of the Latin American distance teaching institutions have struggled to establish themselves as relevant models in their own right and in their own soil must inspire other parts of the developing world in a positive way. It took about 10-15 years for some leading institutions in Latin America to make their presence felt but the efforts were worth making. Oliveira and Rumble (1991) in their review of distance education in Latin America recognise a number of strengths and also point out the weaknesses and constraints of the system of distance education.

The major strength of distance education in Latin America is to be seen in that it "has developed its own forms of distance education to confront realities and problems which are peculiar to the region" (Oliveria and Rumble, 1991). The indigenous forms of distance education, school-equivalency programmes, post secondary in service teacher education, university extension education, mass higher education, rural community education, and many developmental programmes through distance teaching. The progress in these areas had, of course, been made, despite stiff resistance from the conservative circle of academics and policy makers as also the problems caused by paucity of resources, experience etc, which lead to the collapse of a number of programmes and projects. But the success of indigenous models outshines the failures precisely because of the Latin American determination to find its own solutions to its problems and resist the temptation to imitate the European and North American models blindly. In other words, in spite of hardships and some failures, Latin American region has succeeded in creating the suitable forms of distance education through experiment and adaptation rather than adoption of successful models alien to its own reality. This creativity and adaptation can be observed in a number of aspects of the system, including the use of pedagogy and technology. Oliveira and Rumble observe:

> *The successful transfer of the concept rested in part on the use of communication technologies which already existed*

in the region and in part on the decision by the planners to adopt an essentially conservative approach to academic policy, in marked contrast to the British Model…

…In general, the regional development of distance education at the higher education level have been a product of the Latin American situation and not of externally imported technologies, policies and structures.

No wonder, the Latin American region has been able to show to the world such successful institutions as UNA of Venezuela and UNED of Costa Rica.

The mass education programmes organised for the poor peasants by Paulo Freire in Columbia has inspired a number of other countries in the region. The potential of radio had been particularly appreciated by the Latin American institutions in Columbia, Brazil and Nicaragua. Nicaragua's mass educational campaigns in 1979 and the early 1980s soon after the Sandinista revolution were remarkable successes. Cuba has been using distance education as an ideal complement to its face-to-face education system since 1978. From among the Asian countries one could cite Thailand and China as two worthy examples of self-confidence and independent approach in practising distance education in the forms and ways suitable to their respective situations.

From the above survey and analysis of the current practices of distance education in many parts of the world, it should be possible to draw certain conclusions which would have some lessons for the developing countries.

- Distance education will emerge as a major system in the developing world too in the years to come.
- The present practice of adopting the western models will not work in the developing world because of incompatible cultural variations and technological gaps.
- Any attempt to transplant western models in the developing countries will hamper the growth of the system by making it permanently dependent on western experts, technology and teaching-learning strategies.

- There is an urgency to rethink about the current strategies of course development and delivery in all the countries which for some reason or other, have based their strategies on the western, particularly the British model.
- The use of technology needs to be decided on the basis of its access to institutions and learners in the developing countries.
- It is not always necessary to have sophisticated technology to establish successful distance education models in the developing countries.
- Instead of competing with the western models which need heavy investment and high technology, the developing countries should make use of their available resources to meet their specific educational demands.
- To make use of the available resources, the developing countries must develop self-confidence and acquire the ability to think independently when they plan and execute their distance education programmes.
- In order to acquire self-confidence and independent thinking distance educators and policy makers must first study the history of distance education in the advanced countries and relate it to the social and political history of the relevant countries.
- The fixation about the successful western models and the obsession about the inevitability of sophisticated technology must be overcome and a fresh look must be taken at the need and feasibility aspects of large scale use of technology for educational purposes.
- If and when sophisticated technology is acquired by institutions in the developing countries, the use of it must be considered on the basis of its usability and accessibility from the institutional and students' points of view.
- Once indigenous models take firm roots in the native soils of the developing countries, they would gradually emerge as competitors to the western models.
- If the indigenous models fail to take roots, in the era of globalisation educational systems of the developing countries also will soon face the same fate that has been

faced by their economic and political institutions—invisible take over by the multinational and transnational companies backed by the political super powers.

The above conclusions may sound ominous and alarming or even farfetched to those who have been habituated to looking at educational issues in isolation of economic, political and technological developments. But they are not. Distance education itself has become a global phenomenon and its developments have intimate relationship with the developments of global trends in economy and technology. Economic imperialism, political imperialism and technological imperialism have simultaneously forged an alliance with cultural imperialism of which educational imperialism is only a minor component. The dilemma of the developing world is that it has not been able to resist the global onslaught of powerful economies without compromising their own economic interests and political sovereignty. Such compromises are justified by the rulers of the poor nations in the name of 'integrating themselves' with the global economy. In fact, the term ' globalisation' is a euphemism for opening the gates of every country to the economically powerful countries. This is not a voluntary welcome, but a compulsion for the weaker nations without which their very existence as nations would become difficult. The same dilemma, and for the same reasons, is faced by the distance teaching institutions in developing world. It is not a matter of recognition, but a question of resolve that is needed to strengthen the educational models which grow in individual countries much in the same way one feels the need to protect the seeds and plants of different countries which are threatened and destroyed in their own native soils by the patent rights and GATT agreements signed in Uruguay but decided in Washington. .

References

AIU *Handbook* 2001, Association of Indian Universities, New Delhi.

Arger, Geof (1990): "Distance Education in the Third World: Critical Analysis on the Promise and Reality", *Open Learning* June, 1990

Arger, Geof (1993), Distance Education in Asia and the Pacific, Vol.1. UNESCO

Basu, Aparna (1991): " Higher Education in Colonial India" in *Higher Education in India: Retrospect and Prospect*, Ed. Moonis Raza, Association of Indian Universities, New Delhi.

Daniel, John S (1995): "Preface", in *Open and Distance Learning Today*, Ed. Fred Lockwood, Routledge, London and New York.

Dhanarajan, G. (1996): "Key Note Address" to National Seminar on Students Support Systems in Distance Education, IGNOU, New Delhi February 7-8, 1996.

Dunbar, Raden (1991) " Adapting distance education for Indonesians: Problems with learner hetronomy and a strong oral tradition", *Distance Education*, 12(2), 1991.

Government of India (1974) Working Group Report on National Open University (Unpublished), New Delhi. (popularly known as the Parthasarathy Committee Report)

Holmberg, Borje (1989): *Theory and Practice of Distance Education*, Routledge, London & NewYork. ICDL(1999) Data Base, IGNOU Library, New Delhi.

Inquay S (1992): "Distance Education in Ethiopia: A Rejoinder", *Distance Education*, 13(2), 1992.

Laser, W (1995), "Some problems to implement distance education in developing countries", 17th World Conference of ICDE, Selected Papers, ed.David Sewart, 17th ICDE Conference, Birmingham.

Manjulika S, and Reddy, V.V (1996): *Distance Education in India: A Model for Developing Countries*, Vikas publishing House, New Delhi

Miller, Micheal T (1995): "Cultural Considerations in the offering of Courses through Distance Education Technologies", *Indian Journal of Open Learning*, Vol.4 No.1, January 1995.

Mulenga, F.M (1987): "Distance Education at the University of Zambia" *Open Learning*, November 1987.

Oliveira, J.B.A and Rumble, G (1991) " Distance Education in Latin America: A Review", *Open Learning*, February 1991.

Perry, Walter (1976) *Open University*: The Open University press, Milton Keynes, The United Kingdom.

Rumble G (1985): " Distance Education in Latin America: Models for the 80s", *Distance Education*, 6(2).

Sewart, David (1995): Ed. *One World Many Voices: Quality in Open and Distance Learning*, 17th World Conference for Distance Education, Birmingham, 26-30 June 1995.

Smith Peter and Mavis Kelly (1989) Eds. *Distance Education and the Mainstream Croom Helm*. London. New York. Sydney.

Styler, W.E (1984): *Adult Education and Political Systems*, Department of Adult Education, University of Nottingham, The United Kingdom.

2

Technology in Distance Education—Potential, Access and Actual use

> *Given the speed of technological development, and the pressure to use technology for its own sake, caution is essential. Nevertheless, audio visual media are not sufficiently used in distance teaching, primarily because academics and administrators are generally unaware of their potential, inexperienced in their use, or frightened off by their imagined costs.*
>
> – *Tony Bates*

Bates made the above statements in 1984. After seventeen years, one finds his statements still relevant, in spite of the rapid changes taking place in technology and its use in distance education. Perhaps the need for caution and the need to know more about technology before using it are being felt all the more by the institutions which have limited resources for acquiring, and little experience in harnessing technology in distance education.

Educational Technology in Developed World: The Present Scenario

The impressive data available on the flexibility, uses and future possibilities of educational technology make you almost lose yourself in a word of fantasy, and you may as well dream about the power of technology and media. The world created by science fiction seems to become true in the near future even in one's own lifetime. Commenting on the range of media and the swiftness of changes taking place in using communicational technology, David Hawkridge (1995) talks about the possible 'Big Bang' theory in Distance Education within a decade and says:

> *The Big Bang is not so much a theory as a vision supported by much reasoning and speculation about the benefits for students of such a revolutionary change. In particular, exponential expansion seems possible, given sufficient students, because the super-highways would overcome many of the difficulties of supporting these students while they study (p.6)*

He agrees with Duning (1993) and suggests that fundamental changes are approaching with lightening speed, fostered by those who believe in distance education through telecommunications, rather than by educators. The following observation of Hawkridge is quite significant:

> *...While some people think about the Big Bang, others are ready for it (p.6)*

Talking about the reality of the Global Virtual University (GVU), Noel Bridgeman (1999) confidently says:

> *If we are to take seriously the idea of global co-operation for social, economic and practical purposes, then we need a cadre of professionals and a new managerial class as well as scholars and researchers who share a common education and common global skills. It is no longer sufficient to operate at the local level to formulate professional goals in terms of the nation state; the professionals of tomorrow need to understand and deal with global concerns.*

However, the demonstration of the use of technology in a laboratory situation more at the experimental level or as used by a few institutions in some countries is confronted by the stark reality of the developing world with limited or no access to the technological wonders which may very well remain as privilege of a selected few for quite sometime. The selected few may include a few advanced nations and /or certain strata of privileged people in many countries. Access is mostly decided by the questions of ownership, motives and the life span or domination of technology and its innovations. In the unipolar world of globalisation and of undeterred march of the market forces, at least for the present, access to the most advanced technology gets determined by economic, political and military considerations.

Educational and cultural considerations will inevitably become secondary or as an after thought to the overriding principles of economic supremacy, political clout and military domination of nations. Often, only a few or even one nation may determine the degree of access a particular technology should have, however superior the technology may be in meeting the demands of the institutions and nations. The use of technology in distance education also is thus bracketed between the two determinants: availability and accessibility. The potential of the media and technology cannot in any case go much beyond the inspiration that it could cause in educationists, if the access question is not resolved in practical ways. When the potential of modern communicational technology is understood properly, and when technology is made accessible to learners, the actual use of it becomes not only an issue for pedagogy and andragogy but also an issue for budgeting and recruitment.

The recent debates on technology-pedagogy initiated particularly by Otto Peters (1998) and Colin Lomas (1999) are extremely important in developing the right kind of institutional perspectives in the induction and use of sophisticated communication technologies. Technology enthusiasts usually ignore the deeper pedagogic issues and they are generally unaware of the cultural and the linguistic factors playing a key role in accepting and modernising distance and open learning in the developing countries.

Many distance education institutions have been using multimedia technology very effectively where students have access to it. However, in some institutions, the promise to use multimedia educational technology holds good in distance education so far as its 'glamour' value is concerned. This glamour value is justifiable to the extent it motivates the students to join distance-teaching programmes and stimulates them to learn. Reputed institutions offering a variety of courses to a wide range of target groups through distance mode earn their recognition and credibility by making the best of this glamour value. Nevertheless, at the theoretical level the potential of a wide range of technology and media available in whatever degree is very high and, if only the practical problems of accessibility and usability of the same could be overcome, the role of technology will be really revolutionary in changing the very basic principles of teaching-learning.

Sometimes superior technology may be available to institutions but they may not be used fully by the institution concerned or not made sufficiently accessible to students (*e.g.* IGNOU, India). At other places, both availability and accessibility may be there, but the institution may not use technology on a large scale (*e.g.* Fern Universitat, Germany). In some other cases, electronic media may be used extensively and exclusively on a large scale but for specific purposes such as technical and vocational training (*e.g.* China). What kind of technology is needed by distance and open learning institutions is not merely a pedagogic-andragogic question, but also a socio-economic and political question. Therefore, when we talk about relevance, uses, and effectiveness of technology in distance and open learning, we have to consider the *context* in which technology is used.

Technology gap between the Developed and the Developing Worlds

My central thesis is that there is a significant divide between the advanced world and the developing (or underdeveloped) world in approaching the issue of using technology for education.

A few examples of the uses and access of technology in distance and open learning in some of the advanced countries would make my thesis still more clear and convincing. In the context of Canadian distance open learning, Bates (1995) says:

> *We find in 1994 that 74 percent of our students at the open Learning Agency (OLA) had access to a suitable computer for study purposes (up from 37per cent three years earlier)*

The scenarios in Australia and the United Kingdom are also very bright, as far as the access of educational technology is concerned. Kirkwood (1995) says the following about the situation at the Swinburne University of Technology, Melbourne, Australia:

> *Each students will have a personal computer with a CD-Rom, modem, VGA graphics monitor and access to domestic TV, radio, telephone and VCR. Link these everyday items and they can access and communicate with staff and other students at Swinburne and around the world.* (p.130)

As per Kirkwood's estimate the situation in the UK is also very bright. In the UK, 67% households have more than one TV sets; 15% have more than one VCR. The OU students " often have to negotiate a convenient time with other members of the household or wait until everyone else is out or asleep". And that is the problem of access there. But in the poor countries, ownership of even one TV and one VCR is a problem for many households. 'Access' means different things to different people in different contexts.

In the United States of America, Michael G. Moore (1995) observes two clear trends emerging in the use of technology in open learning : a) merging of computer and video-technology which will make the educational technology more interactive and less expensive; and b) satellite delivered programming leading to homogenisation and globalisation of the communication environment. The implications of both the trends shown in the figure 1 are significant:

The trends observed by Moore in the American context are generalisable to other contexts as well, in a greater or smaller degree, depending on the economic-technological growth of nations. It will be interesting to study the correlation between technological dominance of individual nations and their corresponding ranking in the economic, industrial, political and also the military maps of the world. My own hunch is that except Russia and some breakaway republics of the former Soviet Union, every other technologically advanced country would have retained its position, more or less in the same order in its economic and industrial ranking as well, although the same cannot be said about the military strength of nations. For example, Germany and Japan are economic and political powers but not so militarily, though they have the potential to become if they wish to, in a relatively short time. On the other hand, Vietnam, North Korea and Iraq are militarily strong but economically and technologically dependent on others. Notwithstanding these exceptions, as a general rule the economically and technologically powerful usually remain powerful politically and educationally as well. As a corollary, those nations which aspire to emerge as economic and technological tigers must first strengthen their educational and political systems.

Figure 1: *Implications of the Major Trends in Media Technology in Distance Education.*

❑ Computer-Video-interactive media	❑ Satellite delivered Programme
❑ Individual control of Learning	❑ Continuance of group based instruction
❑ More learner autonomy	❑ Greater Stability
❑ Risk of administrative choas	❑ Greater institutional control
❑ Breakdown of old norms of university / academic institution	❑ Reinforcement of the influences of traditional agencies
❑ Leading to virtual university	
❑ Breaking of social control of poor countries technologically advanced countries on the poor countries	❑ Perpetuation of control regime and thus technological dependence of

Derived from Michael Moore's (1995) " American Distance Education : A short literature Review".

In the educational field, particularly in distance education, the use of technology is directly linked with questions related to availability of technology, its access, the cultural environment, and the educational philosophies of nations and individual institutions. For the developing nations like India, the possibilities of reducing their dependence on the developed countries depend on their ability to understand and decide as to what to choose from and how to use the wide range of technology available to them (India's contribution to computer software for example, is very high, but the actual use of computer technology within India, particularly in distance education, is very limited).

Whatever technology is put to use in the advanced countries, it is done so because of, by and large, clear institutional policies and careful planning of curriculum, budgeting etc., and evaluation of it becomes part of the whole exercise. This optimism may be questioned by critical distance educators of the advanced countries for various reasons, but the fact remains that the use of technology there is seen more as a practical need than as something fanciful. Since the changes in technology, including the educational one, take place very fast, there is also a need to update or replace the old and the existing technology. Although it is impossible for institutions even in the developed world to keep pace with technological innovations in terms of change of policies, usually the institutions decide in advance about the duration for which it is used. Additionally, institutional commitment and professionalism of personnel make it possible for the advanced countries to use the available technology maximally, and change over to new technology with relative ease whenever needed and possible. This, however, does not preclude the possibilities of misuse of technology or being caught in the trap of technological determinism that threatens institutions both in the advanced and the developing worlds.

Technological supremacy and the initiative to bring in innovation still rest with the advanced countries. They became and remain advanced countries, precisely because of their supremacy and initiative in the fields of economy and technology. For example, the Open University students in the UK, had access to these technological devices some 10-15 years ago: word processors, broadcast television, video cassettes, satellite, cable, video discs, computers, radio, audio cassettes, telephones, teletext and video data. (Bates, 1984). These are not available to learners in the developing countries in adequate measure.

A number of new technological devices have been added to the above list during the decade that followed. These are : teleconferencing, desktop publishing, home computers, e-mail, voice mail, internet etc. Information super-highways and the Big Bang theories have made it possible the creation of 'virtual colleges' and 'virtual universities', along with virtual classrooms. Therefore, when Bates (1995) envisions the following to happen in open-distance learning, one does hope that the future vision would not get restricted to the technologically advanced countries alone. Bates anticipates the following possibilities of technology for distance education :

- increasing power and sophistication of multimedia computer development, thus rapidly increasing its educational potential;
- dramatic decrease in the cost/power ratio, making sophisticated technologies available to the general public at moderate cost;
- convergence of telecommunications , television and computing, both in terms of technology and business;
- fast-tract developments towards low-cost, on-demand access to digital technologies and services in the home and work place but with public access to technology becoming increasingly fragmented and diverse;
- political moves towards developing public learning networks on the information highway but a lack of policy or strategies by education ministries for the development, application and coordination of educational telecommunications.

The above possibilities throw up new challenges to distance education institutions in the advanced countries. However, these possibilities do not imply that there will be any way of bridging the gap -- technological and others -- between the developed world and the developing world. By the time the costs of the present technologies come down to affordable levels, newer technologies would have arrived in the market, perpetuating the technological gap. Besides these, the overall economic and educational advancement had enabled the advanced countries to anticipate the changes to come with a global perspective, and plan their strategies accordingly in order to withstand global competition and also to safeguard their interest or emerge as dominant partners. This spirit of competition and also the urge to safeguard their interest or emerge as dominant partners. This spirit of competition born of a strong survival instinct makes it imperative for the distance and open learning institutions, too, to keep pace in the race to capture or, at least, retain their educational markets the world over.

Technology - Pedagogy Conflicts

However, using technology for teaching is not a smooth affair even in those institutions where technology is available and accessible. Narrating the experience of the Open University, UK, Hawkridge (1995) says :

> *The fact is that using the new technology for teaching is not a matter of any interest to a considerable majority among present OU academic staff, who prefers to stick to their reading and writing...* (p.9)

The same point was made by John Sparkes (1984) in a much more powerful manner to persuade the technology enthusiasts to involve academics in a meaningful way to make the educational technology really work:

> *If technology can make acceptable and convenient to students, it may not be able to do the same for teachers. Yet it is essential, in the long term, even if not initially, when enthusiasm to experiment is high, to ensure that the methods used are supported by the teachers who have to use them. So, a future factor in education is the problem of ensuring that teachers feel that their time is well spent using educational technology, and that good quality materials and effective teaching is achievable.* (p.218)

Sparkes, however, remembered to caution further :

> *Experience seems to show that educational methods that require very substantial investments of time by the*

teacher soon fall into disuse, once the initial pioneering zeal has passed, unless there are extra motivations for keeping at it. *(p.218)*

Without the participation of the academics and their readiness to use a particular technology, it will not be possible to achieve the desired educational goals in any institution. As Hawkridge (1995) rightly points out :

> *If there is to be general acceptance of the benefits of new technology, academic objectives must be seen to lead rather than follow the technology. Recently, OU course teams have encountered technical difficulties with CD-Rom technology that have placed an extra-load on staff already under pressure.* *(p.11)*

Inducting Technology in Distance Education : Some Issues and Challenges for the Developing World

In the developing world, distance open learning institutions usually tend to imitate or copy the technological models of the advanced countries, ignoring the affordability, usability and accessibility of those models. What works successfully in one situation at a given period of time need not work the same way in all situations and at all times. This simple maxim is often forgotten by policy makers and educational leaders of the developing countries. Caution, scepticism and criticism of the unsuitability of certain western models and technologies in these countries are either overlooked or effectively marginalised by those who have the power. Various unacademic considerations dominate the thinking of institutional leaders when they go for adopting the models, including the technological ones, of the advanced institutions in the developing countries. The first major consideration is to prove that they can do what others can, without looking deeply into the consequences of self-imposed and self-generated challenges such as this. It would be useful to recall what Sparkes (1984) has to say about the pedagogic considerations involved in using technology:

> *The new problem for educational providers, posed by developments in educational technology, is the question of which teaching methods and channels of communication to use, in order to achieve a given set of educational aims. This question does not simply relate to new ways of teaching traditional subjects; it relates to different kinds of audiences, different kinds of subject matter, different kinds of courses, different forms of access to education, as well as to different study patterns amongst those who want to learn.* (p.207)

These considerations, which have much significance in any distance teaching institution are either unnoticed or ignored by institutions in the developing world. The second important consideration is to use the money given to institutions either by the national governments or donar agencies. Institutions, therefore, buy whatever is available in the market. The anxiety and fear of 'losing the funds' impells some to shop around to buy unsuitable technology and dump it in some corner in their institutions. Lack of understanding and lack of foresight of a few individuals could lead to wasting of the limited resources. Because of this basic failure in the understanding of the applications of technology in specific situations, introduction of technology in many educational institutions serves at the best an ornamental purpose or at the worst becomes a hurdle in the educational transaction, which could otherwise be possible through the traditional media such as the print and face-to-face contact sessions. Technology could be used in many instances effectively for administrative purposes rather than instructional processes, if its access is limited.

Besides being ignorant, some of the decision makers may have their own vested interest in choosing unsuitable technology. Technology becomes unsuitable and thus a hurdle to teaching-learning when the institution that acquires it cannot ensure its access to, and use by teachers and learners. The other institutional constraints are : non-availability of professionals to properly handle the media, absence of training facilities, poor infrastructure, lack of appreciation on the part of academics in using the technology and developing the software, lack of incentives or encouragement to the personnel involved and, above all, the absence of suitable environment for creative work. These are all, however, the institutional considerations or constraints in choosing and using technology for education. But what about the access and usability of it from the point of view of distance learners?

By definition, distance learners are not homogenous in many respects: age, education, gender, profession, socio-economic status, learning styles, etc. Because of this very heterogeneity, individualised learning, particularly through multi-media is emphasised and also to a large extent possible in the advanced countries. But this principle literally falls flat in the poor countries.

The first challenge here is that of the number of learners who need education -- the number runs into millions. The next challenge is that of access. Only a small number, comparatively speaking, of rich and urban based students in the developing world can hope to have access to a variety of media and technology used by institutions in the advanced countries. The third challenge is that of familiarity with the technology and the ability to use it for effective learning. Quite often the change over to technological media results in creating psychological stress and anxiety in the user rather than making the teaching-learning process easier. One need only to observe a few sessions of teleconferencing at any distance teaching institution in a developing country to understand the impact of techno-cultural academic shocks which teachers as well as learners have to receive, stomach and digest during their teaching-learning transactions. This cultural change is unavoidable or may be necessary when technology is introduced even in non-educational sectors, but when it enters the educational arena quite a few precautions are absolutely necessary to avoid the possible negative consequences of technological determinism.

A Hypothetical Situation, which could be real in a Developing Country

Imagine a situation where a distance and open learning institution decides to go for multimedia approach in all its educational activities. It must have a variety of media—print, radio/audio, television/video, face-to-face contact sessions at the study centres, telephones, telex, e-mail, fax, internet etc. Besides these, large-scale computerisation and teleconferencing also become necessary, especially when the institution promises to make use of the latest advanced technology for administrative and student support activities.

Poor Human resources

Assuming that the institution has managed to acquire the necessary technology through governmental support and donor agencies, the institution has to address a number of other related questions, which in a rational course, should be resolved much before acquiring technology of any kind. The questions are :

- Are there human resources available to make use of the technology effectively and meaningfully ?
- Are the students ready to use and learn through the technological devices, if the same are made available to them even in a limited way?
- How much of technology, in which areas and for what purposes?
- Are there facilities available to service and maintain the machinery bought by spending a sizeable chunk of money which, in any case, is not available in abundance to the institution ?
- Are there mechanisms to control the quality of the technology processes and to monitor and evaluate their impact on students' learning ?
- Is the institution ready to accept the negative feedback and change its policy to make use of the available technology meaningfully?
- Is the need for training in this are sufficiently appreciated?

Unrealistic Goals

If institutions rush to introduce technology without considering the above questions for the sake of fancy and glamour, or on the basis of unrealistic ambition and expectations, the results will be devastating so far as the institutional health and its future are concerned. Unfortunately, many of the institutions in the developing world have gone ahead with their ' multi-media' approach without adequate preparedness. Availability of sophisticated multi-media technology lures the institutions so much that they get hardly any time to think about the actual educational value of it in a given situation.

The usual arguments put forward by the proponents of multi-media technology is that unless an institution uses technology extensively, it cannot be called a distance education institution. Obviously, the definition of distance is misunderstood and the potential of different media is wrongly estimated in such a situation as the above. Technology is brought in the home market or imported, installed and even operated in a technical sense. Still, the desired goal(s) may not be achieved. How? and Why?

To answer the above questions, it is necessary to consider a few other questions related to the present theme. What are the expectations of a typical distance teaching institution in a developing country? What are the strategies employed to realise those expectations? What about the quality of the products such as radio/audio or television/video programmes? What about the quality of on-line courses/programmes? Can learners be assured of access to them?

The expectations would be somewhat like these :

- Production of audio-video materials.
- Broadcast of the audio-video programmes on the local and /or national networks of radio and television.
- Making available the audios and videos at the regional study centres of the institution.
- Using telephones, fax, telex, e-mail, etc. for effective tutorials, teaching and support services.
- Using computers for both administrative and academic purposes.
- Conducting teleconferences, where the latest technology is available.

Unclear Objectives

To a large extent, institutions in the developing countries may succeed in acquiring the necessary technology for the above purposes and even in operationalising them. But the actual practice may be entirely counter productive. The façade of adopting a multi-media approach may be a device to cover up certain unpleasant realities and bitter truths about the actual use of technology in distance education. Apart from establishing the real need for technology, it is also necessary to clearly define the objectives to be achieved through technology. Both the needs and the objectives must be clear to the teaching staff and the media personnel because they are ultimately the actors who have to perform the acts decided for them usually by some invisible policy makers.

Lack of Professionalism

Where technology is planted without adequate thinking and preparedness, the practical problems doggedly face institutions at every stage. For example, if an institution decides to go ahead with the development and production of audio-video programmes, the first problem it faces is to get the right kind of people for the job. Only those who have reasonable degree of academic qualifications and experience in developing educational programmes can cope with the institutional demands, particularly the demands of academics who care for the quality of content and the educational validity of programmes delivered to students. It is common knowledge that such professionals and those working for the open-distance learning institutions of the advanced countries are not available in good number in the developing countries. This is not to suggest that the educational media producers in the advanced countries are angels or the tensions between the producer and the academics is absent in the institutions there. The point being made here is that at least a reasonable degree of planning, preparation and selection of media academic sensitivity and choice of personnel does ensure an appreciable level of professionalism in these institutions as compared to the self-acclaimed excellence of 'quality' that obtains in the developing countries like India. Lack of appropriate selection and recruitment procedures coupled with non-academic considerations do not allow professionalism to develop in general. Use of technology in distance education is no exception to this malady. Out of compulsion, institutions settle for commercial or young, and inexperienced producers with some promise to do a good job. Under the same compulsion the media personnel go ahead with their tasks without proper training and the necessary planning.

Educational media producers are, by definition, different from the commercial producers. The dividing line is not that of technical expertise but of approach. A commercial producer is usually interested in making his/her products saleable and therefore glamorous. But an educational producer places the primary emphasis on the educational content–the academic credibility, appropriateness of content, authenticity of information and the way it should be imparted to the learner through the medium chosen. Glamour to an educational producer is either secondary or irrelevant. What is glamorous and catchy need not be academically interesting and educationally useful. It is this basic difference in approach to a message of the medium that distinguishes a commercial producer from an educational producer. But when an institution employs commercial producers with little knowledge about the educational programmes, the approach to multimedia teaching learning gets confused and the confusion gets confounded by the unrealistic time schedules and inappropriate arrangements for the actual production. Statistics inevitability triumph over quality.

Need For Training

One way of getting out of this self-created mess will be to train the producers adequately and then ask them to 'produce'. Often it does not happen for various reasons. Appropriate training programmes may not be readily available, or, they may be very expensive. Even when the producers are given the appropriate training, the institution may not be sure of using their training. Or, some producers may leave the institution after getting the training if there are no clear contracts. And if the institutions are not concerned about the cost of training, producers may get 'free' training and use it for other purposes since it may not be obligatory that the training should lead to institutional production of educational programmes.

Absence of Quality Control Mechanisms

If the above hurdles are somehow overcome, and the production takes place, one is not sure of the quality of production. An institution may insist on producing a large number of audio-visual programmes in a very short time to meet the commitments made to the students as well as the government which funds the institution. Meeting the production schedules may not have references to quality or how the schedules must be met. Producers working under pressure of schedules and resource constraints would tend to settle for producing educational programmes, which may not meet the actual academic requirements of the teaching staff as well as the students. Tight schedules may not allow the producers as well as the academics to plan adequately and think creatively. If there is no institutional concern for quality rather than quality of programmes, it may so happen that after spending considerable resources, the producers may just repeat the same academic content available in print in the audio-video programmes too. This happens in the case of institutions, which do not have definite policies on the use of multi-media, or the right kind of staff to work for achieving the intended goals.

Media Policy: Need for Realism and Flexibility

Those institutions which follow the integrated approach to media would naturally insist on specific academic components, which should be covered through particular medium. For example, the UK Open University which adopts an integrated approach to media specifies how much of and what content should be print, radio, television, audio cassettes, video cassettes and other electronic media for each of its programmes/courses. This is done after ensuring students' *access* to whatever media used. The Radio and Television Universities Education (RTVUE) of China, the Correspondence University (KACU) of South Korea, and the University of Air of Japan (UAJ) are some of the other notable examples of institutions having definite policies for multimedia approach in distance education.

However, academic disputes over media policies are bound to exist in any institution but they may not disrupt in every case the general flow of academic communication to the student. Revision of policies regarding technology in open-distance education does take place in the institutions of high repute. Resentment of academics as well as producers over some of the policies and practices of the institutions is very much a common trend but the disputes are of a different nature. And the 'damage' caused by such disputes is containable or hopefully so. In any case, the physical delivery of media materials to the students and the students' access to the materials are not linked with such policies as those which are debated, criticised and evaluated in terms of their economic validity, social acceptability etc. Introduction of any new technology will have implications for the role and functions of teachers and other staff which will therefore be hotly debated in any situation. Knowledgeable debates are necessary to decide initially or revise later the policy related to use of technology in an institution.

In the absence of conceptual clarity and clear policies, one would not know as to what to offer and through which medium. Often, institutions talking about supplementary and complementary policies present a confused scenario, precisely because they fail to tackle the basic questions of access to media– *i.e.* students' access to the media used by the institution concerned. In that case, the students must have the capacity to own the necessary media facilities in some way, even if the complementary and supplementary approaches have to operate, or else, the institutions would divert a sizeable chunk of their resources in producing programmes for the non-print media which may remain little used or unused. If the educational use and value is not ascertained, the electronic media cannot make any significant academic contribution other than serving the ornamental purpose which the distance teaching institutions in the developing countries can ill-afford. The cost factor which is easily noticeable in the case of print materials may be conveniently ignored if the educational use value of the multimedia is not taken seriously.

Paradoxes

Strangely enough, the need for introducing educational technology on a very large scale also exists in the developing countries. The paradoxical situation in these countries is that except the need nothing else is available in any significant degree–advanced technology, the infrastructure and capacity to install it, the human resources to use it or the environment to tape its educational potential. On the other hand, justifications are given by these countries for reducing their expenditure on education. Established open-distance learning institutions which are expected to achieve the hitherto unrealised educational goals by using the modern communicational technology is one such justification. The essence of this justification is the supposed cost-effectiveness of distance education. Even if one accepts it for the sake of argument, is there a way of ensuring the availability, access and use of modern telecommunication technology in these countries ? James W. Hall (1987) understands the irony of the situation with a sense of realism and says:

> *Telecommunication holds the promise not only to fulfill the older notions of university extension, but also to bring to distance education students that quality of education associates with campus-based teaching at its best.* (p.47)

He further says:

> *Ironically, these nations, which have the necessary telecommunications and postal infrastructures, are precisely those in which the needs of students are met most fully by campus based education. Conversely, those nations which most need distance education to reach burgeoning and geographically widespread populations, lack the necessary national telecommunications and infrastructures.* (p.55)

The same view has been expressed by Barbara Martin (1987) while analysing the specific situation of distance education in Kenya:

> *Unfortunately, nations like Kenya, which most need systems of telecommunication technology to teach their growing and geographically scattered populations lack the necessary infrastructure.* (p.70)

She further says:

> *What is needed now are ideas on how the new telecommunication technologies being used elsewhere in the world can be adapted for use in developing countries cheaply and in such numbers that all could benefit from them. .* (p.72)

No wonder that the peripheral educational benefits from multimedia technology get reflected in the academic contributions from the developing countries as well!. In the 17th conference of ICDE at Birmingham, June 1995, there were very few papers from the developing countries on technology used in distance education. In the 'Technology' section of the conference papers, one finds that out of 47 papers only 6 are from the developing world, all descriptive in nature and the remaining 41 from the (so-called) developed world focusing on specific micro issues involved in the practice of educational technology of different forms and at various levels. The breakup of the number of papers is quite indicative of the technological divide that exists between the developed world and the developing world.

The breakup is as follows:

UK	7	Denmark	1
Australia	14	Sweden	1
USA	5	Venezuela	1
The Netherlands	2	India	1
Canada	6	Kenya	1
Japan	1	SA & Israel	1
Hong Kong	1	China	1
Norway	2	Israel	1
New Zealand	1		

Henry C Johnson's (1995) sum up of the challenges to create 'a technology of hope' for distance education in Latin Americas is insightful in the present context:

In sum the situation (social, cultural and educational) in Latin America is now both more complex and more complicated, marked by both vistas of future progress and dangers of regression–which is only to say that it poses both risks and challenges. Who will participate and who will guide (or even control) are still unanswered questions. The process is still uncertain, but the future is also still open. (p.25)

A recent response from Latin America does acknowledge the significant contribution of communication and Information Technology in expanding the operations of distance education in that region, nevertheless it cautions:

But the success of the whole program will depend mainly on the way it is organised to give clear answers to the fundamental concepts of Quality, Pertinence and Innovation (Armengol and Stojanovic, 1999)

A Realistic Agenda for the Developing World

As I am writing this chapter, Delhi, the capital of India is going through a severe power crisis. Offices go without power and light. The entire range of activities come to a standstill, because without electricity computers cannot work, and without light in the office human eyes and hands cannot work, even if the brain is ready to work. Indian situation could still be presumed to be better than most other developing countries of Asia, Africa and Latin America. Imagine as to what would happen if an institution in any developing country insists on the video and two way audio teleconferencing under these circumstances. Experience would show that without uninterrupted power supply, teleconferencing would be meaningless and an utter waste of resources. That is about the technical aspects of this interactive media.

There are academic (both pedagogic and andragogic) issues also which could be equally disturbing. Unless the participation of the intended audience is ensured, and the academic resource persons are properly trained, teleconferencing would simply mean 'ill prepared academics talking to cameras or walls which neither hear nor ask any questions'. One may, of course, take it as an example of effective communication from the teacher to the taught, if one ignores the actual participation of students. At the receiving end there may not be any students either to hear or respond to teacher's message. And even if the students are somehow persuaded to attend the sessions, without developing adequate participative culture and effective communicative skills, they would remain as captive audience who may not get any worthwhile educational 'message' from their teacher talking/performing at the other end of the communicational channel. After a few such ventures and adventures, the institution would find itself in an uncomfortable situation because the laymen and the non-experts may point out the futility of the exercise. In some ways, the exercise may also be justified by 'experts' and the top managers of the institutions because their ' prestige' may be involved and their egos may be hurt when the much publicised technology projects do not take off. In the process of justification, a few more blunders may be committed and the situation may become still worse.

The question is not that of 'using' technology for its own sake just because it is there, but a question of using it purposefully after a thorough preparation. In the case of conducting teleconferencing sessions, for example, a few prerequisites are absolutely necessary: students' access to the media, their ability to participate during the interactive sessions, the infrastructural facilities to accommodate the students, the tested ability of academics who act as resource persons, the academic relevance of the content, and the objective(s) of the whole exercise. If any one of these is missing, then teleconferencing will be a costly exercise which may not achieve the intended purpose. Preparations regarding every aspect of teleconferencing must be thought of much in advance before embarking on the project, without giving scope to discover and rediscover the 'missing components' everytime. An unsuccessful venture of that kind would cost the institution dearly in terms of credibility, and the consequences that follow would have a negative impact on the strategy of teaching-learning through telecommunication technology as such, especially in an academic environment that depends heavily on face-to-face classroom teaching. The conservative, cultural bias against and mistrust of distance education on the part of traditional academics would get strengthened if the experiments with technology for education yield poor results or end up in a fiasco.

The same argument holds good in the case of using audio-video cassettes, broadcasting and telecasting also. If an institution is not clear about its objectives in using any of the non-print media, the choice of any strategy may result in unintended anti-climax. Suppose the students do not have direct access to the non-print media but have indirect access to the electronic media through study centres and regional centres, then, it is imperative to ensure that atleast these centres are accessible to them. The immediate concern in that case is to look at the location of study/regional centres of the institution and the possibility of students coming there to participate in the programmes organised there. The other issues are related to the assistance that the students get and the facilities made available at the study centres. The language as a medium of instruction is another issue. Can a latest educational technology ensure all these?

Let us imagine two situations – one good, and another bad.

In a good situation, the following could be assumed to be happening:

- The institution has acquired a reasonably good range of technology such as computers, telephones, fax, electronic mail, telex facilities and equipment to produce audio-video cassettes, time slots to broadcast on the radio/television network, audio teleconferencing and video teleconferencing facilities.
- It has a fairly good number of talented and competent staff at different levels who could perform their roles with a degree of professionalism and commitment.
- The necessary basic infrastructural facilities such as the equipment, personnel and space at the study/regional centres exist to link the students with the institutions.
- The students are in a position to come to the study/regional centres and are prepared to participate in and learn through the non-print media.

- The language used as a medium of instruction is not a hurdle to receive the content presented and to interact with the teachers/resource persons or the non-print media materials.
- There is proper arrangement for monitoring the performance of the non-print media materials and the teleconferencing sessions.
- The institution has a policy to review, evaluate and modify or change the programmes as well as the strategies from time to time on the basis of the feed back obtained; and
- The institution has the sensitivity to respond to the actual educational demands of the students and therefore has the ability to revise the entire practice of using technology on considerations of its educational worth and resources spent.

In the above situation one could expect the institution to benefit from technology, even if it is not very up-to-date and sophisticated, since, the flexibility to use or reject technology depends on its performance and effectiveness in the context of the developing countries. By evaluating their experiences, the institutions in the developing countries could even build a strong base for introducing more advanced technology gradually.

Now, let us imagine a bad situation, where:

- The institution has money but does not have a clear policy on the kind of technology it needs. (This is different from its ability to buy the technology because someone at the institution wants to have it for what ever reasons).
- By good or bad luck it acquires some of the latest technology through donor agencies, even if the institution does not have the capacity to accommodate, use or maintain the technology (Gifts and donations still hold many in awe and wonder in the poor countries, and the policy makers quite often fail or do not want to see the implications of 'free technology passed on to them).
- Communication units are set up, people are recruited and equipment is installed. But the actual production does not take place as expected because of poor human

resources. The personnel recruited do not have the necessary skills to handle the equipment to tap its potential to a reasonable degree.

- Students are promised that they will have multimedia instructional packages. (This commitment may be made without ascertaining the facilities which students have to have in order to make use of the multi-media).
- In the absence of individual ownership of the necessary hardware such as tape recorders, video cassette players etc. the students have to depend on the study centres to make use of the technological facilities offered by the institution. In that case, students' access to study centres becomes crucial. But since the location of study centres is not convenient to the students, they are not to visit the study centres regularly.
- The students somehow overcome all the hurdles to reach the study centres, but the kind of cooperation and help they except from the staff at the study centres do not come forth.
- Things are badly arranged at the study centres and there is no one to be held accountable because of certain loose administrative policies.
- Students who visit the study centres a few times initially find it difficult to operate the equipment because of unfamiliarity with electronic media. When they view the videos or listen to audios they seem to be thrilled at the new experiences but educationally they do not gain much. For understanding the content and for examination purposes, they still believe that the printed materials alone are reliable. Besides, the language used in the electronic media programmes is somewhat strange, unfamiliar and intimidating to the students whose cultural setting is very different from that of the developers and providers of multimedia packages.
- And as a result of all the above, the students tend to think they do not really miss anything educationally, if they do not visit study centres.

In the above situation, the entire effort to make available multi-media packages to students would either succeed partially, or may go waste. Either way, the institution would have lost much of its resources because investments in multimedia technologies are usually very heavy. Caution, therefore, is all the more important when institutions plan to use technology in situations where they have no previous experience.

The primary question regarding use of technology in distance education is not whether the developing countries need technology because the need exists so obviously and pervasively that any further questions asked in that direction would imply ostrich like conservatism. The real question is: What kind of technology is needed in a given situation? And the related questions are: How is it used or going to be used? Both these questions could be answered only after assessing the overall technological growth and human resource development of a given country. There may be uneven development in the area of technology in some countries which poses fresh problems to policy making, especially at the institutional level. For example, India has the third largest technical manpower in the world and it is among the front line countries in space research and missile technology. It has also become a nuclear power. This advancement does not necessarily reflect the country's overall growth in technology and human resource development. In terms of using the multimedia communication technology for distance learning, India does present an impressive example in terms of technical resources but not in terms of educational use of technology.

Of the 70 correspondence courses institutes (CCIs), only four use radio broadcasting besides print materials. The country wide classroom television broadcasting (1 hour per day, 7 days a week) by the University Grants Commission (UGC) is aimed at general audience rather than specific target groups. The three functional open universities at the state level use audios and videos as supplementary instructional materials. The Indira Gandhi National Open University (IGNOU) uses, besides self-instructional print materials, audios and videos as supplementary materials. It also telecasts 30 minutes programmes to specific target groups through the national television network seven days a week to IGNOU Centres. Of the 600 study centres of IGNOU, for each particular programme certain number of study centres have been activated for tutoring - counselling purposes. The activated study centres are supplied audio-video cassettes relevant to the specified programmes/ courses. Besides these, audio-video cassettes are also available on sale at reasonable prices. But there is no authentic information available on the individual use of these cassettes by IGNOU students. The attendance at the IGNOU study centres indicates roughly 20 percent of the students visit them at least once. The visits include the students' use of audios and videos at the centres. Basu (1994) has documented a number of problems faced by IGNOU students in wiewing/listening to the university's Video and Audio programmes. The point that emerges from the above is that even if distance-teaching institutions in the developing world acquire a wide range of technology, there are number of hurdles in making them accessible to students. These hurdles can be overcome, perhaps gradually, if the institutions in the developing world are prepared to evolve realistic and practical policies of technologies relevant to their needs.

The common assumption shared by distance educators is that the physical distance between the teacher and the students is the biggest barrier that can be removed effectively by using communication technology extensively. Once interactive technology is made available, then the educational transaction takes place smoothly—this seems to be the approach to technology in the context of distance education. But the solution to the challenge is not that simple. There are problematic areas which need far more critical thinking and interrogation than the prevalent untested optimism in order to harness technology in an efficient and meaningful way to serve educational needs.

In the discourse of distance education, technology is of course given a prominent and privileged position, primarily to distinguish distance education form correspondence education. But after a period of time, it becomes necessary to question and evaluate this position of technology in distance education where it is extensively used. And such questioning and interrogation become part of the academic debate which is necessary for a healthy approach towards educational innovations.

In the context of the Australian experiences Danaher and others have developed some significant insights into the contradictory understandings of technology by prominent distance educators (Patric Danaher, Leo Bartlet and Leonie Rowan, 1995). One of their conclusions is that the effect of the contradictory understanding of distance educators with regard to technology indicates the possibility of constructing authentic "conceptions and developments of distance learning curricula, based on a more expansive view of technologies and of their multiple links and relations with curriculum". Responding to the technological imperative in the specific context of Deakin University, Holt and Thompson (1995) identify a number of issues involved in the much-needed strategic thinking in implementing technological policies for distance education. Among others, managing cultures and policies in the technological change process becomes a crucial issue, and the authors argue for "the establishment of an appropriate set of values, beliefs, norms of learning vision". Based on the North American experience, Miller and Husmann (1995) have emphasised the need for developing appropriate technology culture to tap the potential of technology used in distance education. Russell (1992) while talking about the use of television for educational purposes, convincingly argues for the less expensive ways of using the media to achieve the desired goals. He proposes video classroom, as an effective model. Obviously he is talking about the North American experience.

The challenges facing distance education institutions in the developing world include all that exist in the developed world and also some others which are related to the cost factor. The developing countries have to consider the media choice in relation to its impact on the overall cost structure of the distance education programmes. While discussing the Latin American experience Joao Batista Araujoe Oliveria and Graville Rumble (1991) identify, among others, three important factors which limit the use of media : (a) the absolute cost of using the media, including the cost of access to appropriate production and distribution systems, (b) the target population's lack of access to the media used, and (c) the lack of trained personnel to use the media in an educational environment. With certain variations the Latin American experience can be taken as the general experience of the developing world as a whole.

A proper understanding and assessment of the use of technology in distance education both in the developed and the developing worlds should help us evolve a distinct policy and a realistic agenda for the distance education institutions of poor countries. Such an understanding and the assessments would look beyond the potential and the desirability of using the wide range of technology, and would certainly consider the question of access, human resources and the cultural aspect. Cost factor in relation to the educational outcome would moderate the enthusiasm for introducing hi-tech devices to find instant solutions to educational problems caused by deeper social crises. An awareness about the poor human resources and the high cost of technology hardware will persuade us to consider the technology issue from very different angles. Thoughtful policies should emerge, not only to avoid costly risks but also to create an environment where newer ways of using technology may be possible.

References

Armengol, M.C and Stojanovic, L (1999) " Distance Education : A Distance Force For Restructuring the Latin American University". file:\C\\ICDE-Papers\35-Cases Armengol.htm.

Basu, Sisir (1996), " Regular Telecasts by IGNOU: Feedback from Students, "*Indian Journal of Open Learning*", Vol. 5 No.1, January 1996.

Bates, A.W. (1994) " The Growth of Technology in Distance Education" in *The Role of Technology in Distance Education*, Ed. A.W. Bates, Croom Helm, London and Sydney, p.7

Bates, A.W (1995), " Creating the Future : Developing vision in Open Learning " in *Open and Distance Learning Today*, Ed. Fred Lockwood, Routledge, London and New York, p.47

Bridgeman, Neol (1999), " The Global Virtual Univeristy".

Danaher, Patric, Leo, Barlet and Leonie, Rowan (1995) " Interrogating constructions of technology by Australian distance educators", *epistolo didaktika* 1995/1, pp.48-69.

Hall, James W. (1987), " Bridging the Technology–Pedagogy gap" in *Distance Education and the Mainstream* Eds. Peter Smith and Mavis Kelly, Croom Helm, London, New York, Sydney, pp.44-56.

Hawkridge, David (1995). "The Big Bang Theory in Distance Education" in *Open and Distance learning Today,* Ed. Fred Lockwood, Routledge, London and New York, pp.6.9

Holt and Thompson (1995) "Responding to the technological imperative : the experience of an open and distance education institution" *Distance Education* , Vol.16 No.1, 1995, pp 43-64

Johnson, Henry C. (1995), "Distance Education in Latin America : the Challenge to create a technology of hope" in *One World Many Voices: Quality in Open and Distance Learning,* Ed. David Sewart, Vol.1, 17th World Conference for Distance Education, Birmingham, pp.24-27

Kirkwood, A. 91995),"Over the thresold : Media technologies for home learning", in *Open and Distance Learning Today,* op.cit, pp.130;134

Lomas, Colin, (1999), "The Dangers of Disenfranchising the Disadvantaged through Current Developments of Information and Learning Technology (ILT) "or" will the PC replace the teacher or the book?".file//C:/ICDE-Papers\36-Lomascolin.htm.

Martin, Barbara (1987), " Distance Education in Kenya : A Third World View" in *Distance Education and the Mainstream,* op.cit. pp.57-73

Miller and Husmann (1995) "Cultural considerations in the offering of courses through Distance Education Technologies", *Indian Journal of Open Learning,* Vol.4 No.1, 1995, pp. 7-10

Moore, Michael G (1995) "American Distance Education : A Short Literature Review", in *Open and Distance Learning Today,* op.cit., pp.32-41

Oliveira, J.B.A. and Rumble, G. (1991) "Distance Education in Latin America: A Review", *Open Learning,* February 1991.

Peter, Otto (1998) *Learning and Teaching in Distance Education : Analysis and Interpretations from an International Perspective,* Chapter 6, Kogan Page, London.

Russell, Thomas (1992), "Bucking the Trend:" Low-tech Telecommunications", *Indian Journal of Open Learning,* Vol.1 No.1, 1992, pp33-36.

Sewart, David (1995), Ed. *One World Many Voices : Quality in Open and Distance Learning* Vol.2, 17th World Conference for Distance Education, Birmingham, See the selection on "Technology"

Sparkes, John (1984) "Pedagogic Differences Between Media" in *The Role of Technology in Distance Education,* op.cit., pp.207-222.

3

Sharing of Resources : A Necessity for Distance Education Institutions in the Process of Globalisation

The idea of sharing knowledge, expertise and experiences is as old as education itself. In ancient times, scholars went round the world to seek new knowledge and bring back as much ideas and experiences as possible to enrich their native institutions and academic traditions. Scholars travelers and ambassadors during Greeco-Roman periods, the ancient and medieval periods of Indian and Chinese empires and in the age of voyages explorations and renaissance periods of emerging industrial European civilization have left behind them records which clearly show that there had been the practice of sharing knowledge and experience acquired by individuals belonging to different societies and institutions. The modern universities continue this sharing through academics exchange programmes, fellowships, and other visits. Naturally, spread of knowledge and information increased through individuals rather than institutions as a whole. With the advent of modern communication facilities, particularly in the fields of computers and satellites, explosion of knowledge and information takes place on a vast scale and at a high speed. With Internet and e-mail facilities, the academic world has literally shrunk into a global village.

However, sharing of resources in terms of infrastructural facilities, courses, programmes, expertise and human resources started in a distinct form in the recent past with the advent of correspondence education at first and distance/open education now. Proliferation of distance education institutions as well as courses became an accepted norm. Economic argument insists that instead of allocating more and more resources to establish conventional face-to-face educational institutions, we could offer programmes of different types and levels more economically through distance mode. Such an arrangement, it was argued, would greatly facilitate the expansion or democratisation of educational activities, besides saving on the precious resources. By extending the same economic arguments further, it is now being argued that by curtailing unnecessary proliferation and avoiding duplication of efforts, much of the available resources in various forms could be used maximally and more rationally within and across the countries.

The Global Scenario

The concept of networking for the purpose of sharing in distance education has a short history. Networking for the purpose of sharing the limited resources has been conceived and practised in many ways. Individual institutions like the Open University, UK, the Indira Gandhi National University, India and the Central Radio and Television University, China have their wide networks of regional services to cater to the needs of their own students in their respective countries. Where open-distance education institutions in a single country have similar or comparable profiles of students and programmes, they come together to create national networks. The consortia of the USA, the open leaning agency (OLA) of Canada, the Australian network of 8 Distance Education Centres, the Scandinavian Network of distance education and the recent attempts in India to network the open universities and directorates of correspondence/distance education through the Distance Education Council (DEC) are some of the examples of national networks of distance-open learning. With the increasing interaction among the distance education institutions across the world, thanks to the modern communication networking facilities, a different kind of sharing of resources and experiences is emerging.

Besides the age old practice of acquiring new knowledge through academic exchange programmes, the exchange of academic programmes and recognition of courses and credits through accreditation bodies is becoming a reality. In the areas of information sharing, electronic mail and internet are bringing together a number of distance teaching institutions to harness their efforts and energies and use them in more productive ways. Vigorous efforts are on to build resource centres which could cater to the specific needs of institutions, nations and regions.

The commonwealth of Learning (COL), Vancouver, Canada, the International Centre for Distance Learning (ICDL) located in the Open University, UK, the Association of Asian Open Universities (AAOU) and the International Council for Distance Education (ICDE) are some of the international agencies actively involved in the efforts of pooling together the knowledge, expertise, experiences and also the facilities available with the different distance learning institutions in different parts of the world with a view to sharing them. Before we discuss the ways and means of sharing the available resources, let us consider a few basic prerequisites which would make the sharing business meaningful.

In the developed world in general, in North America, Europe and Australia in particular, sharing of teaching programmes, information and research experiences becomes a relatively easy arrangement. The role of electronic media, particularly the computers and the satellite have made it possible for students, teachers and institutions to interact with each other on a day-to-day basis. Correspondence telephones, e-mail, internet, television, teleconferencing, computer conference, audio and audio-graphics are some of the latest technological means through which students and institutions contact each other.

In the United States, for example, tens of thousands of instructional programmes for distant learners are offered by universities, colleges, schools, corporate training departments and the armed forces. "Most of these are delivered by a single teacher using a particular medium" (Moore, 1995). Citing Anderson and Mason (1993) Moore (1995) mentions the Electronic University Networks which offer credit courses on floppy disks for home computers, and through e-mail, on line data searching etc. In both the cases, thousands of students and a number of institutions get linked. In Canada, the Open Learning Agency (OLA) is a well known example of collaboration model. In Australia too, institutional collaborative and networking are on the increase. Micheal S. Parer (1994) mentions three significant examples: the Open Learning Agency of Australia (OLAA), Queensland Open Learning Network and the consortium around the University of Wollongong. Besides, the eight national Distance Education Centres also cooperate with one another to develop distance learning packages in a cost effective manner. The students of Swinburne University have access to European and North American Universities through e-mail and computer networking (Kirkwood, 1995).

There is another form of sharing too. Some of the distance education institutions do not have big physical and infrastructural facilities or a large staff. With a minimum core staff and administrative support, they borrow the learning materials from reputed institutions and adapt them to suit their purpose. The Open Learning Institute (OLI) of Hong Kong (now the open university of Hong Kong), which believes in self-financing has been adapting the materials prepared by the UKOU, Indira Gandhi National Open University (IGNOU) and others from the very beginning (Dhanarajan, 1995). Singapore Open University follows a similar approach. Through the consortium model, a number of institutions in United States make available a variety of courses to many institutions and students. Such arrangements as the above save much of the resources and avoid duplication. Of course, there is always the danger of educational imperialism dominating the global scene in the name of pushing in 'high quality' course materials at low costs. To avoid such dangers, it is necessary to have clear institutional policies to differentiate between a genuine need to adapt and the tendency to borrow because of native inefficiency. Where the institutions have a thorough understanding about the local needs of their learners, they could benefit from the sharing policy because they would know as to what to take and what to reject. The other important point here is the cultural variation which should be given due case in the process of sharing.

The Indian Scene

Distance Education (DE) in India has apparently recognised the educational needs of the people at various levels but certainly has not demonstrated its strength and ability to meet those needs in a meaningful way, precisely because of paucity of resources and relevant experiences. The system being essentially adoptive or derivative, it is still unsure of its potential to claim its rightful place with conviction and confidence as the DE systems do in the advanced societies. DE in India is faced with the paradoxical prospects of a bright future as well as risks and even dangers. The bright future is to be seen in its vast potential and enormous possibilities for DE to grow, and the risks and dangers in its inability to secure adequate resources and gain useful experiences.

To talk about sharing of resources and experiences would mean that we have them both, if not in abundance, at least in adequate measure. But do we? My contention is that till recently we in India had neither adequate resources nor the kind of experiences which could be shared to the advantages of each other. Similarly, the talk of more dynamic DE system implies that there is a dynamic system already! I challenge this uncritical assumption too.

Given the present reality, when we talk of resources, experiences and dynamism, we only wish we actually had them. The distinction between an assumption and a wish is important, if we have to create or generate something that we ought to have. In the context of distance education in India, we are yet to relate and generate the necessary resources and experiences that would make the hitherto toddling DE system walk firmly and possibly make a few strides. Sharing, obviously, will have to wait till we collectively contribute to the creation of resources of the right kind. By resources I mean some thing more than what is popularly understood by that term : Money! Without the relevant resources one cannot really talk of dynamism of whatever variety.

Presumably, the aim of this chapter is to focus on the paucity of resources, the triviality of experiences and the danger of sharing them in their present form. With this caution bordering on pessimism, however, it does recognise the positive developments in the very recent past which, if nurtured properly and assessed correctly, would contribute significantly to both the augmentation of resources and the actual sharing of them. The chapter further argues for the urgent need to generate the necessary human resources, besides the other material resources, lest the system may fall into disrepute. It suggests some of the ways to do that and finally offers a critique of the existing environment that obstructs the dynamic growth of the distance education system.

Paucity of Resources and Triviality of Experiences

At the moment there are about 70 distance teaching institutes/directorates located in the conventional universities, 9 state open universities (of which only 7 are functional) and 1 National Open University in the country. They have admitted about 16 per cent of the total student population at the higher educational level. If we include the private distance teaching institutions catering to the needs of university level learners, the country would have already reached, if not exceeded the target of 16.5 per cent of the total enrolment as fixed by the programme of action 1992 of the National Policy on Education 1986 (Government of India, 1992). If we look at the number of programmes/courses offered by these institutions, one is astounded at the size, variety and operations involved.

For example, the Indira Gandhi National Open University (IGNOU) alone offers about 62 programmes comprising 610 courses in various disciplines, some of them for the first time in the country, to some 700,000 students at various levels. (Vice-chancellor's Report 2001). Dr. B.R. Ambedhkar Open University (BRAOU) offers 14 programmes comprising 178 courses to about 1,80,000 students in Andhra Pradesh; Yashwantrao Chavan Maharastra Open University (YCMOU) offers about 20 programmes comprising 171 courses to 1,30,000 students in Maharastra; Kota Open University (KOU) offers 11 programmes comprising 120 courses to 21,210 students in Rajasthan (DEC-IGNOU 1995). The number of programmes/courses offered by, and the students enrolled in these open universities must be slightly more now when I write this chapter. The other State Open Universities are yet to become functional. Of the 70 odd correspondence/distance teaching institutes (departments/directorates) located in the conventional universities, the enrolments of students in some of the larger ones are worth mentioning. In 1990, University of Madras had 1,12,740 distance students followed by University of Delhi (41,173), Madurai Kamaraj (40,292), Annamalai (37,238) and Mysore (21,332) and the programmes/courses ranged from conventional to non-conventional ones leading to Certificates, Diplomas and Degrees (B. Singh *et al*, 1994). The other distance teaching units located in conventional universities present a wide spectrum in their enrolment and the number of programmes and profiles of students, except the newly established Open Universities and a few Correspondence Courses Institutions (CCIs). One can safely generalise that there is lot of duplication of efforts and squandering of the resources which are already limited in any case.

Every study on the growth and potential of distance education in India invariably bemoans the limited or non-availability of funds, inadequate staff strength, poor infrastructural facilities, absence of staff development, poor student support, lack of monitoring and evaluation, poor quality of instructional materials, limited use of multi media technology, lack of academic leadership and direction, repetition of conventional curricula and courses, inadequate support and direction, from the Vice-chancellors and the Government etc. (Mulay, 1986; Reddy, 1986) A study by Bakhshish Singh (1994 : 74-76) summarises the problems and experiences of CCIs and strongly recommends that they should have, among others, adequate physical facilities, staff strength, research facilities, and media support. For these reasons the study recommends collaboration and networking of CCIs and Open Universities.

Although the Open Universities are better placed in terms of funding and infrasturctural facilities, they too are not in a position to effect any real breakthrough in so far as the quality and the performance of the courses are concerned. It is true that with the establishment of IGNOU in 1985, there have been more expectations of and high hopes on the system. However, better funding and adequate physical facilities alone do not ensure a meaningful change in the system, though money and other infrastructural facilities are basic to any institutional growth and advancement. Given adequate funds and other physical facilities, the only way to bring in changes and reforms in the system appears to be that of acquiring adequate human resources. Though it is not unusual among the academics as well as top executives of distance teaching institutions to quarrel and fight among themselves in various forums on sharing the funds and physical facilities, no meaningful dialogue has taken place so far in analysing, assessing and admitting each other's strengths, if any, and weaknesses which are many.

The general impression about the resource bases of the universities is that they are strong, whatever that adjective means. If the resource bases are strong, they must have yielded tangible results. Outwardly, the open universities, with their better funding and physical facilities are experimenting with a number of activities with a view to translating their mission statements into practical reality. Inwardly, they are suffering as much as the CCIs, if not more, precisely because of paucity of human resources. Obviously, human resources do not mean more human beings. It means the quality of human labour that is necessary to create, recreate and transmit something that money and other material resources alone cannot do. In the context of Indian Open Universities, money, and to a large extent other physical facilities are also available. But one cannot say with confidence that the same is true of human resources.

For example, IGNOU launched its Bachelor's Degree Programme (B.A., B.Com) in January 1988. By December 1995 the programme completed 8 years. The first batch of students would have completed the maximum period allowed to them to complete the programme But only when one looks at the completion rate, it will be possible to say whether or not the material resources have led to better performance of programmes/courses. Admittedly, many factors contribute to the better performance. But the fact remains that availability of the right kind of human resources is a crucial factor for desired outcome. One way of finding the answers related to the quality, performance and effectiveness of IGNOU courses would be to evaluate the courses and also the human resources which developed those courses. Such an evaluation becomes urgent because,

> *The course materials provided by IGNOU are rated to be of a very high standard and some of their programmes have earned international reputation. But 20% of the students in the formal stream of the Bachelor's Degree Programme (BDP) find the course units much above their levels of comprehension.. Obviously, the percentage of such students in the non-formal stream who do not have the requisite entry qualifications must be still higher. Probably, bridge courses in different disciplines and simplification of the language of instruction might help such students to come up to the level of other students who find the course units good or even very good (B.Singh et al, 1994).*

Course evaluation becomes all the more imperative in the context of sharing, adopting or adapting the materials of IGNOU by other open universities and CCIs. Validating of the courses would clearly tell us more about the quality and relevance of resources and experiences available in the different teaching institutions as well in India. I have given here the IGNOU example only to emphasise the simple fact that the human resources are absolutely necessary to make use of the other resources purposefully. Mere sharing of material resources does not necessarily lead to success in distance teaching. For various reasons distance teaching institutions in India did not take staff development and professionalism seriously. Whatever excuses may be given for not doing so, the fact remains that most of our academics even today are not required to acquire professionalism. The reasons could be many and they may be probed and debated separately. In the context of sharing the resources, recognition of our weaknesses and constraints will help us know better and become wiser in using the limited resources and facilities when they are pooled and shared. Since 1962 we have done very little in this direction, although the system has expanded in quantitative terms.

Sharing of Resources: The Experiences of Others

As we said at the beginning of this chapter, sharing and networking in distance learning are taking place nationally and internationally. But the quality of sharing and the terms of sharing use be thoroughly scrutinised: Since we readily borrow anything from others, there is no harm in borrowing some good practices of others too. Sharing of resources, information, knowledge and experiences takes place mainly through networking and cooperation. Europe presents numerous examples of efficient networking leading to interaction among institutions within individual countries and also across the continent. National, geographical, linguistic and even political barriers get silently broken with networking of knowledge. In the days of information super-highways, traditional isolation and insularity of institutions become great disadvantages to even the greatest institutions which prided in their uniqueness and individuality. The shift from isolation to integration becomes easier through telecommunications, satellite communication and computer networking. Distance teaching institutions in Europe, the United States, Canada, and Australia seized the initiative and also the opportunities, as they usually do, and have come together to share their resources and experiences. Their sharing helps their institutions, not only in improving their own programmes but also in flooding the educational markets of the developing countries with their technology and programmes or ideas. Globalisation in the real sense is taking place in the advanced countries to their advantage. By the time we in India start talking about sharing and networking, our counterparts in the developed countries would have gone ahead of us with two or three decades of rich experience and expertise. And we shall, because of our late awakening, continue to depend on others for everything, notwithstanding our hollow patriotic slogans.

The first major European network for distance education—the Association of European Correspondence Schools (AECS)—was started in 1968 with 60 member institutions from 16 countries. In 1987 the European Association of Distance Teaching Universities (EADTU) came into existence with 5 open universities, 6 consortia groupings, the National Distance Education Centre of Ireland and the DIFF of Germany. With its member institutions in 12 countries EADTU represents about 50 distance teaching institutions of different types. SATURN is another European network with 80 member institutions from 13 countries. SATURN encourages partnership between industry, commerce and distance teaching Education (EuroPACE) sponsored by 11 companies. In 1988 it had 140 members from 15 countries. EuroPACE porgrammes are based on satellite transmission with a feedback system that uses telephones, telefax and electronic mail. In 1989 The European Association of User of Satellites in Training and Educational Programmes (EUROSTEP) was founded and it has more than 100 broadcasting members from 20 European counties (ICDE, 1991). EDEN (the European Distance Education Network) established in May 1991 is now a network of about 170 institutional and individual members from almost 30 European countries. By "special agreement between EDEN and ICDE, EDEN serves as ICDE's main European Partner Organisation " (Blom.D., 1995).

In Canada, the Open Learning Agency (OLA) is a well known model of cooperation that has successfully brought together leading Canadian open learning institutions to share their instructional materials, resources and experiences. There are other networks too. The Beacon initiative, a joint project to upgrade local, regional and national network of multimedia communication will make broadband capabilities available to 80-90 per cent of businesses and homes, including educational institutions by 2005. By 1999, researchers and educational communities across Canada will be connected through the Canandian Network for the Advancement of Research, Industry and Education (CANARIE) (Jennifer *et al*, 1995). Besides these telecommunication and research networks, Canada has strong computer networks and educational consortia, too. Similar networks exist in Australia, the United States, the United Kingdom, Norway, Sweden Finland and other individual countries of the developed world.

In the case of developing countries, networking and sharing of resources are much delayed. Although UNESCO, UNICEF, and of late the World Bank and the Asian Development Bank have funded a number of projects, sharing of resources has not really taken roots for the simple reason that the institutions and individuals who got the funds have created very little knowledge to share. The most important developments in the direction, however, are the establishment of the Commonwealth of Learning (COL) in 1988 and the formation of the Asian Association of Open Universities (AAOU) in 1986. These two agencies have made significant contributions in bringing together many distance teaching institutions in the commonwealth (and Asia, in the case of AAOU)

Recent Efforts in India

In India, the idea of sharing through networking of some sort, has been there for quite sometime. The idea had been expressed by distance educators and policy makers on a number of occasions when they came together during the conferences, seminars and workshops. However the first major step in sharing the infrastrucural facilities started with the location of study centres of IGNOU mostly in the conventional colleges throughout India. This was followed by YCMOU which established its study centres and work centres. With the establishment of State Open Universities in many states, this trend shall continue, and it will be easier for the State level open universities and other distance teaching institutions to share the local facilities more effectively than for the National Open University to do so. As a matter of fact, the CCIs of Madurai Kamaraj University and Madras University in Tamil Nadu have been using the facilities offered by the local colleges for quite some years. As regards sharing of courses, IGNOU course materials have been used through adoption or adaptation by Maharastra Open University (YCMOU) and Kota Open University (KOU). With establishment of the Distance Education Council (DEC) in 1992, the idea of pooling the courses and other resources of all the open universities and the CCIs is gathering momentum. And with the establishment of the Staff Training and Research Institute of Distance Education (STRIDE) in 1993, the possibility of generating the necessary human resources indigenously has become real. The Electronic Media Production Centre (EMPC) of IGNOU is another resource centre which promotes sharing of its resource by many institutions.

Sharing of resources and experiences among distance education institutions in India is possible through many ways. However, the following need immediate attention to demonstrate our will to share:

- Sharing of multi-media instructional materials after proper validation (DEC could play the pivotal role in this).
- Using the available staff development programmes to train the academic and non-academic staff at the distance education institutions (STRIDE has been engaged in this for quite sometime).
- Using the available human resources effectively and meaningfully. There are about 2400 persons with Diploma/Post Graduate Diploma in Distance Education (PGDDE); and about 350 with Masters Degree in Distance Education (MADE). The programmes were developed by STRIDE and offered by IGNOU. Both the programmes have been internationalised through the Rajiv Gandhi Fellowship Scheme sponsored by COL, Canada by admitting 100 students from 18 Commonwealth countries. The scheme is likely to be extended further. Between 1999 and 2001, more than 100 students from Africa were admitted to PGDDE under the IICBA-UNESCO-STRIDE-IGNOU collaboration scheme.
- Making use of the existing study centres and work centres of open universities and CCIs (IGNOU alone has about 400 study centres spread across the country).
- Using the library facilities available are the study centres of open universities, conventional universities, colleges and research institutions.
- Taping the multi-media resources available with IGNOU, the EMRCs, AVRCs, UGC and other multimedia centers.
- Using the available telecast/broadcast time on the TV and Radio in the national network as well as the regional services.

- Using wherever possible, the audio-video teleconferencing facilities now available with IGNOU and DECU of ISRO.
- Establishing common printing, publication and distribution facilities at the national and the regional levels.
- Linking up with educational publishers to make available essential readings to distance learners at affordable costs.
- Collaborating with conventional educational institutions and research laboratories for the use of the lab facilities by distance learners.

One can think of many other areas of cooperation and collaboration among distance teaching institutions as well as the conventional institutions. With the faster introduction of communication and information sharing technologies, the distinction between the 'distance' teaching system and the 'conventional' one is getting blurred. And if the distinction disappears sooner, the better. But to first effect sharing of communication, information and, through them, the resources we need a sound database and a computer networking with e-mail and internet facilities, if not. Whereas the private sector is thriving on e-mail, internet and other means of faster communications, educational institutions, including the distance teaching institutions in India display an astonishing degree of ignorance in investing in the relevant technology and using it with efficiency. There are institutions which have made huge investments in computers and information technology but do not know how to use them properly. There are others who do not go for anything beyond the typewriters. Obviously lack of proper policies and absence of trained human beings must have contributed to this kind of romancing with or shying away from technology. Also there are institutions which suffer from the dog-in-the-manager policy: Neither can they use their own resources, nor will they allow others who can use them. From the above analysis of available resources we could safely assume that we have, at least now, a fair amount of material resources and some degree of human resources. Of course, we should aim at augmenting them further. The real question is not one of sharing them but that of using them meaningfully.

It is basically a question of attitude that helps or mars the possibility of bringing institutions together to pool their resources and share them purposefully. To effect the attitudinal change in individuals is perhaps the most difficult task. Still, we can attempt that. Attitudinal changes usually follow the changes in environment. But in order to change the environment for the better, it is necessary for the individuals, especially those who have authority, power and influence to realise the need to change their attitudes and implant some basic changes in the environment.

Possible Areas of Sharing in India

The major difficulties faced by developing countries in educational sharing are in developing adequate human resources, infrastructural facilities and the administrative and managerial skills to make use of available resources. Because of paucity of human resources, developing countries face hurdles even to utilise the limited facilities made available to them. These include the training they receive from the developed Western countries, the technology they receive from others either as donations or at low costs and the programmes designed and developed for them by the consultants from the UK, USA, Canada, Australia and other developed nations. The key to the success of educational as well economic programmes in the developing countries is the development of human resources locally. Some of these countries have made efforts in this direction in recent times. Thailand, Malaysia and South Korea have shown to others how, with a little effort and creative labour, indigenous systems of distance education can be developed successfully.

In India, although correspondence/distance education has been practised since 1962, very little has been achieved in offering programmes in a professional way (Ramanujam, 1995). However, after the establishment of the Indira Gandhi National Open University (IGNOU) in 1985, a number of efforts have been continuously made to improve professionalism of distance educators and also the quality of programmes. Some of the significant changes that have taken place in the Indian distance education landscape are in the areas of staff development,

development of self-instructional materials in print and non-print media and the students support services. In all these areas the impact of IGNOU is clearly seen perhaps more by the non-IGNOU staff than by he IGNOU staff themselves.

In the first two areas, the contribution of the Staff Training and Research Institute of Distance Education (STRIDE) (previously the Division of Distance Education) needs to be emphasised. Although there is little appreciation for the work of STRIDE in some quarters of IGNOU itself, the definite impact of the activities of STRIDE both within and outside IGNOU becomes evident if one asks two simple questions:

- What was the state of staff development in distance education in India prior to 1987 (*i.e.* before the STRIDE (Previously Division of Distance Education) started its activities?)
- What was the status of distance education course materials before IGNOU materials arrived on the scene?

Untill the IGNOU launched its Diploma in Distance Education in 1987, there was no comprehensive professional staff training programme in distance education in India. As a matter of fact, the need for staff development was not recognised by the Correspondence Courses Institutes (CCIs) located in the conventional universities. The low status accorded to the staff working in CCIs was deplored by Review Committees and Expert Committees on correspondence education but very little was actually done to change the situation (Reddy 1986; Singh 1994; Mulay 1986). Keeping in view the paucity of human resources in distance education in the country, IGNOU entrusted the responsibility of developing appropriate training and professional programmes to the then Division of Distance Education. The Diploma in Distance Education was the outcome of the efforts of the Division of Distance Education. Besides launching the full-fledged professional Diploma programme, the Division had also simultaneously started organising training programmes of varying durations for the academic staff of IGNOU, the State Open Universities and the CCIs. About 12 intensive workshops were conducted by the Division of Distance Education between 1986 and 1991 with assistance and participation of UNESCO, ODA and other agencies besides conducting a few hundred (about 500) short-term orientation-cum-training programmes for course writers and counsellors (about 600). As of 1999, STRIDE has conducted about 50 workshops of 5-10 days duration.

In 1993, on the basis of the recommendations of three Review Committees of the Commonwealth of Learning (COL), Canada, and also the general recommendation of the Asian Development Bank (ADB) in its Islamabad conference in 1989 to set up a Regional Training and Research Centre of Distance Education for the region, which was fully supported by the Indian Government, the Division of Distance Education was upgraded as the Staff Training and Research Institute of Distance Education (STRIDE). Thus STIDE was created with the active support of the Commonwealth of Learning, Asian Development Bank, the Government of India and the IGNOU.

In 1993, STRIDE started offering Masters Programmes in Distance Education and from 1994 the postgraduate Diploma programme in Distance Education has been on offer. In all, there are three professional programmes on distance education offered by IGNOU, and all the three are pioneering creations of STRIDE in the area of staff development. Recognising the importance, quality and appeal of these programmes both at the national and the international levels the Commonwealth of Learning (COL) conferred the status of Centre of Excellence in Training in Distance Education on STRIDE which is usually acclaimed as a recognition of the entire IGNOU as a centre of excellence (Pollard's Report, 1995). If all the human resources developed by STRIDE could be taped meaningfully, distance education system in India would make a significant progress in terms of quality and quantity. But forces within IGNOU are actively involved in marginalising and punishing STRIDE for its better performance.

Rajiv Gandhi Fellowship Scheme

Whether the potential and use of the STRIDE programmes and its activities have been adequately appreciated or not within India, external recognition to these programmes has been steadily growing. After the COL's recognition of STRIDE as the centre of Excellence in Training, under the Rajiv Gandhi Fellowship Scheme, 100 students from 18 commonwealth countries registered for STRIDE's Master Programme in Distance Education. Indications are that more countries would opt for STRIDE programmes in the future, provided STRIDE is able to get adequate staff and infrastructural facilities to cope with the growing demand. Of the 100 students, 61 have received their M.A degrees in Distance Education. The second offer of this scheme begins from January 2002.

IICBA (UNESCO)-STRIDE(IGNOU) Scheme

In 1999 at the request of the International Institute for Capacity Building in Africa (IICBA), an UNESCO body, and STRIDE (IGNOU) entered into an agreement to make the PGDDE and MADE programmes to African countries. Ethiopia, Liberia and Madagasear together have enrolled about 100 students for PGDDE. More African countries will join this scheme soon.

The Indian Journal of Open Learning (IJOL)

Indian Journal of Open Learning (IJOL) is one of the six referred international journals in the field brought out by STRIDE since 1992. It has been widely acclaimed as a forum to generate and disseminate knowledge, research and information about the on going programmes of distance education in India, with a reasonable space to accommodate the contributions from the other countries. IJOL is emerging as a strong forum for discussions, interaction and debates on distance education in the developing countries.

Training Programmes

The most important contribution of STRIDE is to be seen in the areas of design, development and production of self-instructional materials. Curricula for the various programmes of IGNOU which are delivered through multimedia were basically designed on the broad principles of curriculum design developed by STRIDE for the Diploma in Distance Education Programme. Almost all the units of IGNOU courses in print had passed through the hands of the educational technologists of STRIDE. A handfull of units developed by some individual faculty members also followed the same self-instructional format for IGNOU materials—the format developed by STRIDE. More than 500 orientation-cum-training programmes for the course writers of various disciplines of IGNOU programmes and near about 600 orientation-cum-training programmes for counsellors — the academic counsellors in the IGNOU context — had been conducted by STRIDE staff. In this way about 5000 senior academics who wrote units in different disciplines and about 11000 academics staff at different levels who work as Academic councellors at 400 study centres of IGNOU throughout the country have been trained or oriented to contribute to he development of the system. In addition, 600 odd coordinators and assistant coordinators managing the study centres of IGNOU have also been oriented to distance education through a number of orientation programmes organised by the Regional Services Division and the distance education component of these programmes was supplied by the STRIDE staff. In course of the 75 training-cum-orientation programmes organised by STRIDE for the non-teaching staff at the IGNOU headquarters and the 17 regional centers, about 850 persons have been oriented to understand the specific needs and demands of the system and respond to them in a professional way. The seven IGNOU Handbooks developed by STIRDE on the different aspects of Distance Education became handy for all the above purposes.

At the international level too, STRIDE staff have made contribution to the development and sharing of human resources. Mauritius, Maldivies, Bangladesh, Sri Lanka, Bhutan, Ethiopia the Middle East and Myanmar had sought STRIDE expertise to develop their programmes in distance education. In the course of implementing Rajiv Gandhi Fellowship (RGF) scheme, about 20 Academic counsellors in 18 Commonwealth countries have been trained by STRIDE so as to develop local human resources in the developing countries of the Commonwealth. The counsellors trained by STRIDE will act as resource persons in their own countries or region in implementing distance education programmes in the 18

Commonwealth countries covered by the RGF scheme. If the human resources and training materials already developed by STRIDE could be properly used and shared, it will go a long way in meeting the human resource needs of India and other developing countries. The only questions are : whether there is the necessary will to recognise our own professional base and competence? Whether we have the wisdom to use that base internally and then extend the expertise and services to others who need them?. Given the strong base that exists at IGNOU in the form of STRIDE for creating and developing human resources at different levels of distance learning operations, India can be expected to meet the training needs of the developing countries in the field of distance education.

Distance Education Council

Distance Educational Council (DEC) was created in 1992 within the overall management of IGNOU to partly act as the agency to network distance education institution within the country and also to perform the role of the apex body assigned to IGNOU by the Act. Through networking DEC would pool the resources available at the national level and help the institutions in sharing the available resources rationally. DEC is a statutory authority with representation from the Union Ministry of Human Resource Development, Department of Education, the State Open Universities, Directorates of Correspondence Education and IGNOU. The Vice-Chancellor of IGNOU is the Ex-officio chairman of DEC (DEC-IGNOU 1995).

IGNOU has a dual role to play : to act as a National Open University and to function as the apex body to promote, coordinate and determine standards of distance in the country. The second role is to be carried out through the mechanism of DEC. During the last four years of its existence DEC has made efforts to develop guidelines on the following:

- Data base on distance education institutions programmes/courses, personnel and the available literature in the country.
- Common pool of courses/programmes for sharing by open universities.

- Support to State Open Universities to develop human resources.
- Norms for mutual recognition of programmes, courses and qualifications in consultation with the University Grants Commission (UGC), All India Council for Technical Education (AICTE), Association of Indian Universities (AIU) and National Council for Teacher Education (NCTE).
- Norms for common pattern of students assessment, credit transfer and quality assurance.

DEC, when fully and properly activated, will play a significant role in improving the quality of distance education as well as its promotion. Both are possible if the present resources are pooled and shared on a rational basis. Much of the duplication of efforts and wastage of resources at the distance education institutions in the country could be avoided. And they can be avoided through appropriate legislation, leadership, coordination, networking and cooperation. Kulandaiswamy (1995) observes that the distance education system in India " can function more effectively and more economically if it pools its resources". To drive home the same point he gives the following example:

> *If you take Tamil Nadu, the three giants in distance education are : Madras University, Madurai Kamaraj University and Annamalai University. All of them offer B.A., and M.A. courses in many subjects that are common. If you take, for instance, History or Commerce, I do not think that there is any major difference in the curriculum and syllabi among the universities for the major subject, i.e. History. Today, each of the three universities writes, prints and produces its own course material. It can be prepared at one of the universities with participation from others and printed in large numbers and used by all the three.*

Similar is the situation in the rest of the CCIs of conventional universities offering distance education programmes, the State open universities and the National Open University.

If cost effectiveness is one of the main planks of distance education, then, pooling and sharing of forms of resources is necessary. The immediate danger as perceived by institutions and the staff in this arrangement may be loss of jobs, funds and autonomy. This may happen, if the present approach to the quality of distance education and student support services continues. But it need not be the case. When the institutions and the staff take quality issue seriously, without any possible loss of jobs and autonomy, they can benefit more through pooling and sharing of resources, and more attention could be paid to improve the quality of services. All these are possible if DEC could creatively use its statutory powers with the necessary cooperation of the UGC, IGNOU, the state open universities and the CCIs.

Electronic Media Production Centre and Other Media Units

In the area of sharing the learning materials in the non-print media, there are a number of agencies and units, functioning in isolation or independent of one another. The Electronic Media Production Centre (EMPC) located in the IGNOU is one of the most technically well equipped units in Asia for the production of learning materials in the audio-visual media as well as transmission of educational activities through satellite based telecommunication. With about Rs. 80 crore investments the EMPC has the latest equipment of the electronic media and infrastructure. With a committed leadership and professionally trained production staff to tap the potential of the centre it can play a major role in transforming the present one way distance teaching into a two-way interactive open learning. The EMPC (previously the Communication Division) has so far produced about 1050 audios and 1120 videos to supplement the IGNOU programmes/courses which are mainly offered through the print medium. The UGC's Countrywide Classroom telecasts 1 hour television programme seven days a week for the school children through the national television network. Programmes for these telecasts are usually produced by the 4 Educational Media Research Centres (EMRCs), 8 Audio-visual research centres (AVRCs), and the Central Institute of Education Technology (CIET), but quite a few are also borrowed and if invested in all these media production centres are pooled and shared on scientific lines, perhaps the cost be improved. Another important arrangement for the purpose of promoting cooperation and collaboration among Educational Media Organisation with emphasis on distance education is the Commonwealth Media for Asia (CEMCA) established by the Commonwealth of Learning (COL) Canada, which is located in IGNOU (IGNOU : A profile 1996).

Concluding Remarks

Some important conclusions could be drawn from the above discussion. Sharing of resources, experiences, knowledge and information in distance education has become a global necessity. Developed countries have been responding to this necessity through their efficiency and aggressive marketing. Developing countries therefore, cannot remain aloof from this practice. Although the resource bases in the developing world are still fragile, there are signs of significant progress in some of the areas such as the human resource development, especially in India. The absence of a culture to think along scientific lines with a long term perspective hinders the process of developing and sharing appropriate resources in the developing world. Practical demonstration of sharing the available resources in a more meaningful way even in a few countries, would inspire others, and develop self confidence in them to think and act appropriately to meet their specific local needs which cannot be met by the recipes of successful models either of developed or developing countries. The success of sharing is to be seen in the ability of a developing country to recognise its real needs in distance education, identify the sources of support and use the available support to meet those very needs through successful implementation. To bring in the above cultural change in the developing world may be a challenge in itself and a long term goal. But the challenge has to be met and a beginning has to be made, if bigger goals are to be achieved.

The experiences of North America, Western Europe and Australia are valuable in their own socio-academic contexts. An understanding of these experiences, however, is necessary for any developing country to put into appropriate practice the principles of sharing and networking in its own specific socio-cultural context. Without an understanding of the available experiences, developing countries would be wasting their time and energy reinvesting the wheel. At the same time, thoughtless imitations and copying of western models in this area too will be counter productive. With necessary caution, institutions of distance open learning of the developing world should collaborate and interact with their counterparts with a view to enriching their own academic base without becoming eternally dependent.

The environment in India to develop and sustain a strong educational system has not emerged so far. The necessary political will and proper material support to build a system of education that is suitable to build a modern, democratic and secular nation are lacking. The size and complexity of a country like India cannot and should not accommodate straitjacketed models or cut and dried policies and dicta's to impart relevant education to the millions of learners who are in need of different types of education at different levels (Renga Ramanujam, 1995) Independent India has been witnessing all these years a strange mixture of genuine aspirations and dithering political as well as academic leaders who have not been able to keep their promises to put education in the priority list of nation building. As a consequence of this, educational investments are misused or simply wasted. In the absence of political will and academic leadership, the environment will not change for the better. One only hopes that the present political promise to allocate 6 per cent of the GNP will at least be kept during the Ninth Five Year Plan.

Political will gets demonstrated in the allocation of budget and in providing other infrastructural support for Education in general and Distance Education in particular. The superficial talk about cost effectiveness and cheaper ways of spreading education to the masses should not become a justification for curtailing the state subsidies for Education in a situation where privatisation has no social obligation. The various aspects of 'cost' must be understood first before we talk about its 'effectiveness',

If the distance teaching institutions have to counter the onslaught of privatisation of education in the name of globalisation and efficiency, it becomes imperative for distance educators to assert themselves as first rate educators; and for this purpose they have a rightful claim over the necessary resources. Leaving the dubious argument about 'academic freedom' etc. they should first make themselves accountable, not to some petty bureaucrats managing the administrative units of educational institutions, but to themselves, the students and the people. Once that happens, they can count on the support of the people to demand more resources for education, training and research.

When academics resist the moves to marginalise their role in shaping academic policies, they at the same time, have to fight for quality education. Cheap education in the economic sense should not become a mediocre one which, I am afraid, is right now the only one available to the less privileged and the socially disadvantaged sections of the Indian population. That the situation is the same in other developing countries of Asia, Africa and Latin America cannot be a solace to us. (For a discussion, see Laser, 1995). The short term goals of saving on education will spell disaster in the long term in the face of global competition, information revolutions and knowledge explosion. The only safeguard for us in the present reality is to invest more in education and share the resources among educational institutions through cooperation with a view to enhancing quality learning. For the same reason, distance teaching institutions must come forward to share whatever limited resources they have, and strive to secure more in the days to come. That can happen, if we ourselves are able to take the initiative, instead of waiting for miracles to happen.

References

Blom, Dangny (1995), "Cultural and social aspects of new technologies in education: A European perspective : in *One World Many Voices : Quality in Open Learning*, Ed. David Sewart, 17th World Conference of ICDE, selected papers, 1995, Vol.1., pp.18-19.

DEC-IGNOU (1995) *Open Universities in India – Academic Programmes* – IGNOU 1995.

Dhanarajan, G., Swift, D.F. and Hope A.(1994) "Planning for Self financing at the Open Learning Institute of Hong Kong" in *Economics of Distance Education : Recent Experiences*, Ed. G. Dhanarajan, Hong Kong.

IGNOU (1995), IGNOU: *A Profile*, New Delhi.

IGNOU (1995),Vice Chancellor's Report to the Sixth Convocation, New Delhi.

Kirkwood, Adrian (1995), "Over the threshold : Media Technologies for Home Learning" in *Open and Distance Learning Today*, Ed. Fred Lockwood, Routledge, London and New York.

Laser, W. (1995), Commenting on the limited resources and periodical cuts in funding of distance education institutions in the developing countries, says : "As a consequence institutions have to lower their recurrent costs by cutting down teaching staff employed at the central institution, by offering relatively poor tutorial and counselling services and by reducing the quality of learning material. Drop-out rate then increases and the efficiency of the system is considerably affected." W. Lasser (1995), " Some problems to implement distance education in developing countries", 1995, 17th World Conference Papers. ICDE, Vol.1, pp 303-306.

Ljosa Earling (1991), " Distance Education in Europe and Models for Organising Future Co-operation ", ICDE *Bulletin*, Vol.25, Jan.1991.

Moore, Michael (1995), " American Distance Education : A Short Literature review" in *Open Distance Learning Today*, Ed. Fred Lockwood, Routledge, London and NewYork.

Mulay, Vijaya (1986), *Reports of the Committee on Correspondence Courses*, University Grants Commission (Unpublished)

O'Rouke, Jennifer *et al* (1995), "*Distance education in Canada: 1995" 17th World Conference of* ICDE, *selected papers*, 1995, Vol.1 pp.28-29

Parer, Michael S. (1994) *Unlocking Open Learning*, Centre for Distance Learning, Monash University, Australia

Ram Reddy, G. (1986) *Ivory Towers Thrown Open*, Sterling Publishers, New Delhi

Renga Ramanujam (1995), *Reflections on Distance Education for India*, Manak Publications, New Delhi, Chapters 2 & 3.

Singh, B. *et al* (1994) *Correspondence/Distance Education in India : An In depth Study*, Ed. B.N. Koul, Indira Gandhi National Open University , New Delhi.

4

Organisational Structures and Work Culture of Distance Education Institutions

> *The formulation of policy is by popular consent, a matter that should involve the maximum of participative democracy. The implementation of policy cannot efficiently be carried out by the same process.* Sir Walter Perry

The Structures of traditional or conventional face-to-face educational institutions of higher learning such as colleges, universities and advanced centres of learning have fairly well established conventions and norms. A university offering residential courses will have three basic human components: students, teachers and administrative/support staff. Of the three components, the students constitute the most visible and vibrant one in any face-to-face teaching - learning organisation.

Norms and conventions of behaviours of students, teachers and the support staff in a traditional university are also well known. While the students go in search of teachers and knowledge, the teachers impart their knowledge and skills to their students in various ways in formal and informal situations. The support staff do not claim any dominant role in running the university except in asserting their rights to safeguard their welfare and professional or career interests provided for in the overall scheme of university structure, governance and policies. They play a supportive role to enable the teachers and the students perform their respective roles effectively. This pattern has evolved over the past seven centuries, particularly in Europe and it remains more or less the same in the conventional universities throughout the world.

Similar uniform pattern is observable also in the physical structures of the campuses of conventional universities: classrooms, administrative buildings, students' hostels, playgrounds, and residential quarters of the teaching staff, libraries, laboratories and recreation centres. Besides these physical structures the organisational structures and the mode of governance too follow near uniform patterns with the senates, syndicates, academic councils, boards of management, executive councils etc., with proper representation of teachers, students, parents and/or the governments. The composition and the actual functioning of the governing bodies may vary in details but not so in substance, since they operate within this frame work of university autonomy, though in recent times the universities of the developing countries are fast losing some of their traditional academic and functional freedom mainly because or their over dependence on state funding or internal weaknesses of the academic communities. Nevertheless, the established patterns of governance and behaviour in the conventional universities continue to sustain the basic work culture where each individual knows what he/she is expected to do.

In the context of distance education institutions, the major human components (*i.e.* the students) being away from the campus life, the conventional pattern of behaviour, organisational structures, and the governance get substantially altered, although the semblance of university structure and governance still exists in the parlance of administrators of distance education institutions. Because of the absence of students as a collective community and a force, the organisational culture is essentially determined by the remaining two categories only : the academic staff and the administrative/ support staff with various sub-categories. The very numerical ratio of academic and the administrative/ support staff places certain restrictions on the numerically smaller academic staff in exercising their power to shape policies, norms, rules, behaviour pattern and the work culture in a distance teaching institution, notwithstanding the dominant role formally assigned to them to do the same. What at first appears to be an "adjustment" in the change of role of teachers as 'academic managers' to carry out the different forms of educational transactions, gradually becomes an activity of a very different kind where without the cooperation of the different categories of staff, teaching - learning cannot take place.

A distance education institution resembles a big industry or a commercial firm in its operational aspects. Because of the high degree of division of labour and a range of inter-linked operations demanding team work, the individual activity of a classroom teacher gets absorbed in the act of distance teaching-learning. This basic difference between classroom teaching and distance teaching further alienates a distance teacher from the conventional image about himself as a teacher. His role also undergoes a change: from the position of a 'teacher' he becomes an academic 'manager' or a 'facilitator' who makes arrangements that are necessary for learning to take place. Having accepted this change of role, the distance teacher looks for the appropriate institutional environment that would allow the teamwork to go smoothly. However, the frictions and clashes start exactly at this juncture in a distance education institution.

Sir John Daniel in his keynote address to the Pan Common Wealth Forum in Brunei in March 1999 highlighted the rapidly changing roles of academics both in the distance and campus based Universities thanks to the developments in communication technologies. Though his views are extremely important and thought provoking as they are, they don't, however, address the fundamental difference between a classroom teacher who still retains his academic authority as an individual and distance educator whose individuality inevitably gets dissolved in the teamwork of distance teaching. This difference is extremely important when we discuss the changing pattern of university teaching vis-à-vis communication technologies as well as university structures.

The organisational structures of distance education institutions are necessarily different from those of their conventional counterparts. Centralisation and decentralisation of powers, functions and responsibilities become simultaneously important and inevitable. At every stage, the organisational structures have to respond appropriately to the needs of the staff as well as the students. Since the students are physically away from the institution, the academic and the administrative/ support staff are called upon to work in tandem to make the teaching-learning process interesting and meaningful. The organisational structures, therefore, have to be basically democratic, if high level of cooperation and teamwork have to be ensured. If structures become bureaucratic and hierarchical in all the functional areas, then, the first casualty will be the team spirit—a loss which will lead to the abandoning of the institutional mission as such.

But the difficulty in creating democratic culture in distance education institutions arises not so much in creating formal structures of governance and administration as it does in actualising the democratic process at the policy formulation and the implementation levels.

If the first Vice-Chancellor of the first Open University in the UK had problems with democracy in the implementation of policies that were otherwise democratically formulated, he has at least one enviable freedom: The freedom to listen to everyone and ultimately make up his mind and take his own decision (Perry 1987). But the subsequent developments in distance education in the UK and elsewhere do not allow the chief executives of distance teaching institutions to wield greater powers. At least in theory, the governance of teaching institutions is vested in the statutory bodies and the Vice-Chancellors are to run the universities in accordance with statues and ordinances and the provisions made thereof. In the case of dual mode institutions, the Vice-Chancellors are mainly tied up with face-to-face/campus based teaching and the responsibility for running and implementing distance teaching programmes rests with the Directors who hardly have any powers. The conflict between a democratic aspiration and the implementational difficulty often results in unsatisfactory work environment and at times virtual stagnation. Can there be some solutions?

Organisational structures exert direct influence on the attitude and the efficiency of different categories of staff working in distance education institutions. They, thus, ultimately determine the success or failure of institutions in achieving their goals. An analysis of the structures of these institutions would indicate the degree of autonomy the institutions enjoy and a further analysis of the composition of governing and administrative bodies would reveal the strengths and the weaknesses of institutions in creating appropriate work culture.

In this chapter I propose to consider mainly three types of distance teaching institutions in India and their typical problems with structure, governance and work efficiency. The three types are:

1. Directorates/Departments of Distance/Correspondence education located in conventional universities;
2. State Open Universities with greater autonomy to design and implement their programmes in accordance with local needs and
3. The Indira Gandhi National Open University (IGNOU) with a dual responsibility– *i.e.,* as a teaching university and afs the apex body to coordinate and determine the standards of distance education in the country.

At the end, I consider the case of the UK. Open University and compare it with the Indian with a view to demonstrating the work culture vis-a-vis the Open University structures in the two different situations.

The National Open University (IGNOU) has an international character as well, since it admits students from Commonwealth countries to some of its programmes. For example, IGNOU'S Distance Education Programmes, PGDDE and MADE, are offered to 105 students from 18 Commonwealth countries under the Rajiv Gandhi Fellowship Scheme in collaboration with the Commonwealth of Learning (COL), Vancouver, Canada. In addition, programmes in Computer Science, Management and Commerce are offered to students in the Gulf region.

The different mandates, responsibilities, resources and jurisdictions of above mentioned three types of distance teaching institutions presuppose difference in their structures of governance, policy formulations and implementation of those policies. Obviously, participative democracy has to be viewed in each situation, keeping in view the possibilities and the constraints. The desirability of any given practice in this regard must be viewed in relation to its effectiveness in an institution of similar nature.

The organisational model of the Open University, UK, could indicate the comparative merits and the demerits of the model in the context of India as well as the developing world. Let me first consider the Indian models.

Type1: Directorates/Departmentsof Distance/Correspondence Education

There are about 70 dual mode institutions of the above type in India located in various conventional universities, deemed universities and other teaching institutions. The governance and the structures of these institutions are anything but autonomous. Their structures are more or less similar. Basically the departments are located in the conventional institutions. Usually, the departmental heads are similar to the heads of other departments of the mainstream institutions, although the heads of distance education departments are sometimes called Directors. Their powers are limited and they have hardly any freedom to formulate or implement their policies, programmes etc., related to distance education independently. A few representative illustrations from this type will make it abundantly clear the kinds of problems the existing structures of governance of these institutions throw up. A typical department/directorate of the type under discussion has the structure as per figure (Jose Chander, 1991).

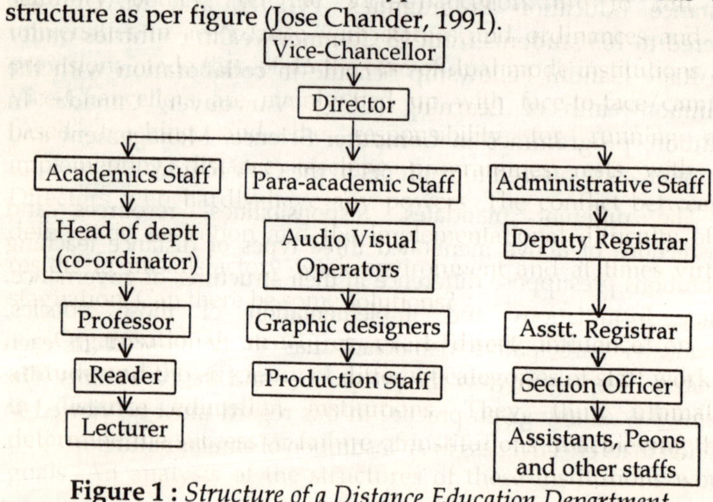

Figure 1 : *Structure of a Distance Education Department*

Most of well known directorates such as the ones located in Madurai Kamaraj University, Madras University, Andhra University, universities of Kerela, Calicut, Mysore, Punjab, Sri Venkateshwara and others have similar structures. The overall governance rests with the university and the special needs, problems etc., of the directors hardly get any attention. Reddy (1986) and others have discussed at length the problems of such institutions from the point of view of governance and autonomy.

The School of Correspondence Courses, University of Delhi, the Department of Distance Education, CIEFL, Hyderabad and the Directorate of Distance Education, Himachal Pradesh University have slightly different structures with a resemblance of functional autonomy. The School of Correspondence Courses (now the Open Learning Campus), University of Delhi, for example enjoys the status of an affiliated college, functioning under the overall supervision of the Executive Council of the University. However, the Managing Committee which looks after the day-to-day management and administration of the school has representation from the Executive Council as well as the staff of the School. The arrangement allows greater freedom for the School to manage its academic and administrative affairs without having to wait for the permission from the University authorities on every issue as is the practice in the case of other directorates of most universities. The Department of Distance Education, CIEFL has sufficient internal freedom to plan its curricula, and select its students, study materials and delivery system.

The above variations in the structures of governance, however, do not alter the basic character of the institutions of this type, the basic character being that of minor players with less or no autonomy, although most of them are in reality treated as the financial reserves and hinterlands of financial inflow by the mainstream departments. Participative democracy, therefore, does not practically exist in this type of distance teaching institutions. The only advantages they have is to find an easy excuse for all the ills afflicting the directorates/departments and put the entire blame on the lack of autonomy. What is lacking in these directorates is a collective effort and an urge on the part of the staff to wake up from the present slumber and demand more autonomy from within to revitalise their academic activities.

Type 2 . State Open Universities of India

Eight state open universities have been established by the State (provincial) governments of India primarily with a view to freeing distance education form the clutches of unimaginative administrative control of the conventional institutions/ universities. This is an impetus to distance education so far as the formal autonomy is concerned. The real challenge, however, has been the ability of the State Open Universities to take advantage of their hard earned autonomy and build their academic credibility on par with the established, conventional universities of academics repute. The nine open universities at the State level have been established by Andhra Pradesh, Rajasthan, Maharastra, Bihar, Madhya Pradesh, Gujarat, West Bengal, Uttar Pradesh and Karnataka. Here I shall consider only two cases: Andhra Pradesh Open University (now Dr. B.R. Ambedkar Open University) and the Maharastra Open University or YCM Open University. Andhra Pradesh Open Universiy was the first Open University in the country (henceforth Dr. B.R. Ambedhkar Open University). Established in1982, it has the following as part of its mandate:

> *To complement the programmes of the existing universities in the State in the field of higher learning so as to maintain the highest standards on par with the best universities in the country.*
>
> *To promote integration with in the State through its policies and programmes (V S Prasad, 1992)*

The Ambedkar Open University has the structure of governance as per Figure 2.

The YCMOU or Yashvantrao Chavan Maharastra Open University was established in 1988. The mandate given to the university includes the following aims:

> *To make higher vocational and technical education available to large sections of the population.*
>
> *To give special attention to the needs of the disadvantaged groups, in particular people in the rural areas and the women.*

To relate all courses to the development needs of individuals, institutions and the State.

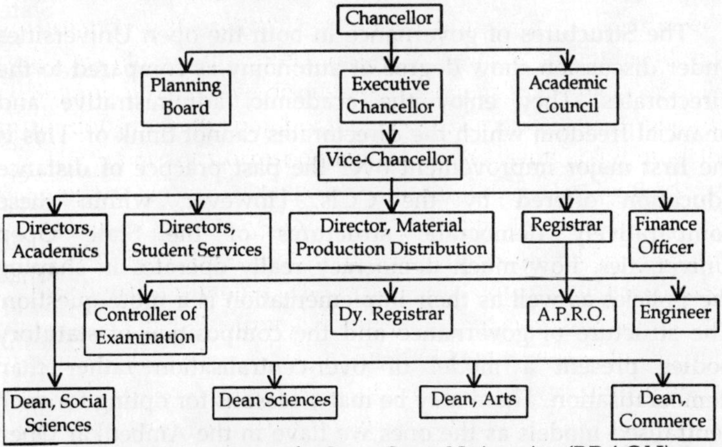

Figure 2: *Structure of a State Open University (BRAOU)*

The university makes some of its courses available both in English and in Marathi, the local language. The University's major thrust is expected to be on applied, technical and vocational courses. The University proposed to operate in a cost-efficient manner and make efforts to become self-sufficient in its operational costs within the first five years, *i.e.*, by 1994. The YCM Open University has the similar structure as the Ambedkar Open University of Andhra Pradesh.

Certain features standout very prominently in the structure both the State Open Universities:

Their jurisdiction is confined to their respective States.

Their concerns are of local nature and therefore they have to be launching programmes to meet the local needs.

The programmes are offered in English and wherever possible in the mother tongues of people belonging to the States.

The possibility of using the mother tongues as media of instruction is more in the State Open Universities especially when unconventional courses/programmes are to be launched.

To meet the educational demands of the States, the open universities should have appropriate structures of governance and autonomy (P.M. Deshpande, 1992).

The Structures of governance in both the open Universities under discussion show degree of autonomy as compared to the directorates. They enjoy the academic, administrative and financial freedom which the directorates cannot think of. This is the first major improvement over the past practice of distance education offered by the CCIs. However, within these comparatively democratic structures of the State Open Universities, how much democracy really operates in shaping the policies as well as their implementation is a mute question. The structure of governance and the composition of statutory bodies present a model of over-centralisation rather than democratisation. There may be many reasons for opting for such centralised models as the ones we have in the Ambedkar Open University and the Maharshatra Open University. We shall consider some of the reasons for this choice a little later.

Type 3. The National Open University

The Indira Gandhi National Open University was established in September 1985 with the following two major functions:

1. to function as a university and
2. promote, coordinate and determine standards of distance teaching institutions in the country.

The simplified version of the structure of governance at IGNOU is shown in Figure 3.

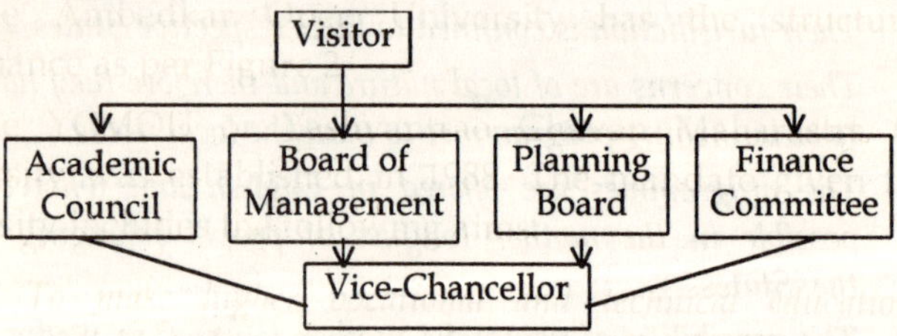

Figure 3: *IGNOU Governance Structure*

The Board of Management, the Academic Council, the Planning Board and the Finance Committee are the statutory authorities of the University.

Let us consider the four authorities of IGNOU one by one.

The Board of Management consists of 14 members. Of the 14 members, only 5 are from IGNOU. Of the five, the Vice Chancellor, and the senior most Pro-Vice Chancellor, are ex-officio members. The other three are nominated members. Of the three, one is a Director of a School, and the other is a Director of a Division (RSD). And so there is only one member from among the teachers. But he is also a nominated member. On the contrary, 9 members are from outside the University, most of them being Vice-Chancellors, government nominees or persons with executive powers in their own organisations.

The Planning Board consists of 16 members of which only 5 are form IGNOU. Of the five one is the VC, one is the PVC, one a Director of a School and two are nominated members from amongst Teachers of IGNOU;. 11 members are external.

The Academic Council consists of 26 members, almost double the number of each of the two authorities referred to earlier. Of the 26 members, 16 are from IGNOU and 10 from outside. It is a clear deviation that allows more participation by the internal members of the University. Of the 16 members of IGNOU, except the VC, the PVCs and Registrar, the rest are Teachers from Schools. Obviously, the internal participation and the academic components are more in the constitution of the Academic Council than that of the other authorities of the University.

Finance Committee is relatively small in size consisting of 7 members of which three are from outside. Virtually it consists of the government functionaries, and the top management of IGNOU. Thus, it leaves no scope for academics to have any say in the financial management of the University.

For all practical purposes, the four authorities usually endorse the proposals of the Vice-Chancellor. Where there are cases of dissent, the VC can always carry out his plan by a majority of the members in each of the various statutory bodies, particularly the BOM. But in practice, it is the VC who usually has the final say, of course, generally in accordance with the Act, statutes and ordinances. The unlimited power of the VC flows from the very constitution of the authorities, and it is the same source of the VC's utter helplessness at times. Walter Perry (1986) laments that the position of the Vice-Chancellor of the UKOU in statutory terms " is in a position opposite to that of a harlot, and holds responsibility without power". But it need not be the case in every situation.

Besides the above four authorities, there are at least four standing Committees, viz., Establishment Committee, Purchase Committee, Students Services Committee and Works Committee. There is one more authority of the IGNOU that is, the Distance Education Council, different from those of other authorities of IGNOU, and therefore, we shall not discuss it here. For the present purpose, it will suffice to confine ourselves to the four authorities and the Schools and Divisions of the University.

Schools vis-à-vis the Four Authorities of IGNOU

Schools of Studies are supposed to be the mainstay of the various academic activities of the University. The Divisions are expected to lend support to the Schools in their activities at all levels. At present, there are nine schools of Studies (the establishment of the tenth one is under active consideration) and some of the schools have many disciplines under them. Each discipline has the statutory provision for core staff, and each school is headed by a Director who is a Teacher of the University.

Almost all the academic programmes which are on offer were decided by the university with the approval of the Board of Management when practically there were no full-fledged Schools or disciplines. It is understandable, considering the initial stages of the University and the compulsions at the stage. As of today, the courses/programmes are proposed by the Schools through the School Boards, which are considered later by the planning Board and the Academic Council and approved by the Board of Management. Once the proposals are approved, the Schools concerned initiate the development of courses/ programmes. In the development of courses, the internal faculty as well as the outside academics are involved. The degree of involvement varies from School to School and within Schools from discipline to discipline. Since the only major activity for the academics so far has been that of course development, any assessment of their involvement, their productivity etc. has to be made in comparison with the creation (output) of courses/ programmes only. Such an assessment is yet to be made in order to see the relationship between the structure and the work culture of the university.

Certainly, the constitution of all the four authorities of IGNOU are top heavy. Within the top heavy structure, the internal participation is minimum, except in the case of the Academic Council. Where you have more outsiders as members of governance, you will have more areas of conflict and disagreement in deciding about the course of development of your own organisation. But the idea behind having more outsiders on the governing bodies of universities in India is apparently to account for the public cause such as education and the desire to account for the public money spent on education. This is understandable, and even welcome. However, if we consider the specific cases of Open Universities, this justification may not be acceptable, unless the external members are reasonably familiar with the specific features of distance and open learning.

In the governing bodies of conventional universities, inclusion of outside academics and experts as members would not pose serious problems for the simple reason that the general issues and guiding principles related to universities will be the same. There are some issues specific to a university which may be dealt with in the light of the experience of 'conventional' academic administrators. In the case of Open Universities the inclusion of members who are otherwise eminent but do not have much exposure to distance and open education system or any new curricula will create more problems in the governance than solve them.

If we look at the over-all structure of various authorities of IGNOU, it will become clear that the top heavy structure is one of the reasons for internal conflicts adversely affecting the work efficiency. This is so because the actual participants do feel that they are not a party to the decision making process, and therefore they are not accountable for any failures and set backs.

Except the Academic Council and the School Boards, the rest of the authorities have more external members than the internal members who are actually and directly involved in the activities of the University. Where the academics are more in number, they have powers only to recommend and supervise the academic programmes. Practically they have no say in the administrative activities and the financial management of the system. Since all the academics in open universities are to be engaged in academic as well as administrative activities, they need to have greater say in shaping both the academic and the administrative policies of the universities. The very nature of the functions at an Open University makes it obligatory and in many cases necessary that academics also act as "managers". They have to manage and supervise the whole range of operations within the university, and , to the extent they are involved in the student support services, also outside the university. Such a responsibility of an open university academics is very different from that of academics of 'traditional' or conventional universities. Therefore, it is necessary to critically examine the governing structure of the open universities and see whether the existing structures are efficient or not, in attaining the goals set before them.

My contention is that except the internal members *i.e.* the Vice-Chancellor and the other members who are employees of the University, others rarely show much interest in the affairs of the University. Even when they show interest, it may be for reasons other than actually helping the open university and the distance teaching system. For, example, the members who are the representatives from the government may be worried about overspending on certain items which the university may feel it is absolutely justified considering the unique nature of the operations. Members who are not sufficiently oriented to distance and open education may tend to compare an open university with conventional universities and often resist any deviation from the norms meant for conventional universities. Budgeting, staffing, student support services, media policies and a host of other issues specific to open universities are usually approached with conventional ideas. Or the members may not evince much interest at all!

Two consequences follow from the above situation.

1. If the members take a negative view of the proposals put before them, the Vice Chancellor and other internal members will have difficulty in carrying out even the best proposals, because of the numerical strength of the outside members, or
2. If the members do not show much interest, the proposals from the top management of the university, however detrimental they may be for the university, shall be carried out.

In either case it does not augur well for the university. The plea, therefore, is that the composition of the Board of Management/Executive Council and other statutory bodies of an open university should be such that persons with knowledge about and experience in the unconventional mode of education should be more in number. The membership should be based on the knowledge and administrative experience in the open university system. And the constituencies of the internal membership must be expanded and filled with persons who have maturity, understanding of the system and the ability to visualise the shape of things to come in future. It is important that every statutory body must have representatives of students and other stakeholders.

If we analyse the very structures of an organisation and its various sub-units, we could also identify the essential traits of the administrative/functional culture. If the structures, for example, are over centralised/political, the organisation may show quick results in the initial stages but will eventually come to a standstill due to over straining or inertia. If the structure is bureaucratic, some of the routine tasks may be carried out very efficiently but further creative development of the institution as well as the personnel may be very difficult, if not impossible. If the structures are democratic, and the work force is carefully selected, then, perhaps, there will be mutual trust as well as satisfactory work output too. In the absence of the above three types, we have one more option: organised anarchy. In smaller units, the last model may be good, but in vast organisations it may very soon turn into mere anarchy.

My own view on this is that centralised models are the easy options left before policy makers and administrators, particularly the Vice-Chancellors who are expected to show quick results with minimum resources. Because of lack of enlightened academic traditions, democratic culture and professional commitment, the modern universities, including the Open Universities cannot simply be managed in a collegiate manner. This, in my view, is the single most important reason why centralisation is possible, preferred and recommended by the government as well as the chief executives. To democratise the Open Universities—this may be true of all Universities in India, for that matter—one should start with building up of academic credibility, respect for democratic norms and a positive attitude towards work. When pressure builds up form below, the top management inevitably gets democratised out of compulsion and necessity. Till such a change takes place, the centralised structure of governance of open universities shall continue to be viewed, if not by others, certainly by the insiders as a master—slave model—the master being the top management and the (mental) slaves being the staff!

Ramona A. Bitter (1999) while emphasising the need for relevant research for Latin America observes that "identifying and recognising our limitations is the first step on the way to growth". This is equally true of research into the structures and governance of open universities as well. Unless we do some comparative educational research in this area, we will be unaware of our limitations and strengths and we will be reinventing the wheel every-time.

Organisational structure and work culture of the Open University, UK

Indira Gandhi National Open University of India, Allama Iqbal Open university of Pakistan, University Terbuka of Indonesia and a host of other open/distance teaching universities have liberally borrowed from the Open University of the UK. Many of the policies and functional mechanisms of these universities are modeled after the OUUK. Course team approach to prepare multimedia instructional materials, students support through regional networks, the concept of counselling, tutoring, credits, credit transfer, modular approach, etc. are some of the notable aspects of the OUUK which have been adopted by many of the distance institutions in the developing world.

However, in adopting the democratic structures and the work culture of the OUUK, the institutions in the developing countries seems to be very reluctant. It is a peculiar practice of borrowing some formal structures and general polices of success models, without adhering to their real spirit and built-in culture that the developing countries actually suffer from. Where formal structures, devoid of their inner substance become the dominant features of institutions, decision making becomes more and more centralised, leading to alienation and frustration of individuals. This process eventually leads to poor work culture among staff. This also encourages and legitimises the autocratic and hierarchical tendencies in decision making.

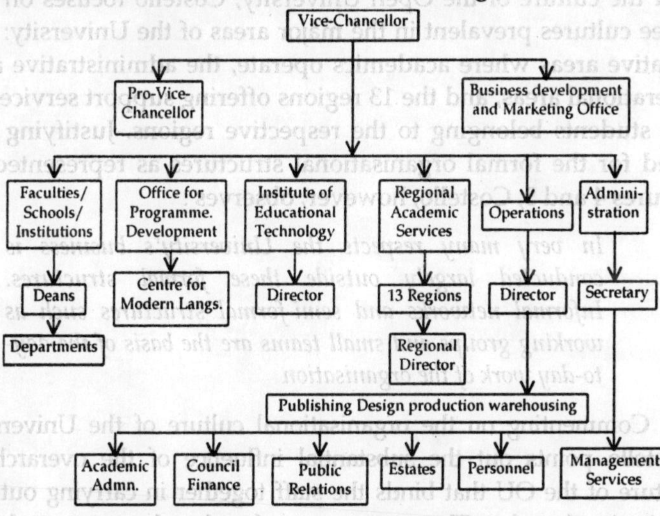

Figure 4 : *Simplified Open University (UK) Organisational Structure*

The continuous success of the Open University, UK has been guaranteed by the basic democratic structures of the university and also by the loyalty of the staff to the institutional mission. Let us look at the organisational structure of the Open University, UK as simplified by Neil Costello (1993)

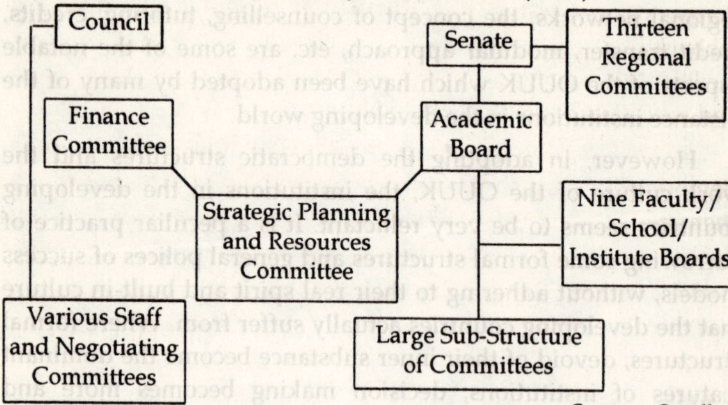

Courtesy: Costello

Figure 5: *Simplified Open University (UK) Organisational Structure*

In a research study of the distinct, organisational structure and the culture of the Open University, Costello focuses on the three cultures prevalent in the major areas of the University: the creative areas where academics operate, the administrative and operational areas, and the 13 regions offering support services to the students belonging to the respective regions. Justifying the need for the formal organisational structures as represented in Figures 4 and 5, Costello, however, observes :

> *In very many respects the University's business is conducted largely outside these formal structures. Informal networks and semi-formal structures such as working groups and small teams are the basis of the day-to-day work of the organisation*

Commenting on the organisational culture of the University, Costello points out the substantial influence of the overarching culture of the OU that binds the staff together in carrying out the institutional tasks. The strong set of cultural norms and the symbolism of the university as a democratic community are demonstrated in many ways. For example, there is "no distinction made between categories of staff or students in the provision of facilities on the main campus", and "even in the most hierarchically structure parts of the university access of senior managers is seen as a right which all employees can assert" (Costello, 1993). Such strong democratic cultural norms as these naturally would not allow lobbyists, coteries and bullies to twist rules and norms to garner facilities and benefits as seen in institutions with hierarchical control and weak democratic culture.

Since the predominant culture of the Open University is democratic, issues are put on the table, debated thoroughly, and then the decisions are taken. As the potentially controversial decisions or unusual decisions are taken the ultimate measure of value being service to the students, the staff are loyal to the University's mission.

In the so-called creative areas of teaching and preparation of course materials, the academic staff follow the culture of' 'adhocracy' for the reasons of flexibility and freedom. This adhocracy, however, does not minimise the self imposed discipline of the academics who strictly follow tight schedules. The staff work in small teams, where power is based on expertise of individuals who apply their power in informal ways. Though the Deans and the Directors have strong formal powers, management is usually and essentially through consent and persuasion. In spite of all these positive, democratic traits, the creative areas "have been the only ones to lose staff since 1985" as Costello says, because of the increasing strain on resources to appoint more staff. As a result, the existing staff have to accept more work load which has implications for their parity of esteem and work with their conventional counterparts.

The operational and administrative areas where large scale specialisation and standardisation are required the tasks are "managed by direct supervision in a relatively hierarchical way" or individual professionals are allowed to work to the "norms and values of professional culture". On the whole, the cultures of both the bureaucrats and the professionals do not deviate from the "founding principles" of the University. The culture of the regions too conforms to these founding principles, though the regional staff do have the feeling that the centre is uncaring because of bureaucratic inertia. The overarching culture comprising multiple sub-cultures of the university therefore cannot be monolithic, if it has to be democratic.

Despite the democratic culture and the team spirit for excellence, there are problems and risks. In the creative areas for example, as Costello observes, " the desire for independence is faced daily with the urge to interfere". Besides, because of academic alienation and absence of direct feedback from the students, many academics take resource research, or simply opt out. These negative traits, however, have not so far affected the University's culture substantially.

By and large, the above democratic culture operates in the western Europe, North America and Australia. It is only a matter of documenting the details of individual institutions in countries such as Germany, France, Spain, Sweden, Canada and Australia of course, the local variations in policies and practices are very much a reality in the open distance learning institutions in the countries. For example, the strong academic traditions insistently influence the curricula and instructional processes of the Fern Universitat of Germany. Structurally it is very different from that of the UK Open University. The Open Learning Agency (OLA) of Canada is more of a consortium of a network of fullfledged distance teaching institutions. The eight centres of Distance Education in Australia brought under the Open Distance Learning Association of Australia (ODLAA) operate within the dual-mode universities of Australia where the same teaching staff who teach the on-campus also teach their distance learners too. In Sweden and Canada, because of the demographic and geographical factors individual case of learners is assured in the very structure of the institutions, particularly with regard to students support services. Enormous amount and freedom and flexibility are allowed to the teaching staff, tutors and counsellors. All this goes on to prove the simple fact that organisational efficiency is inseparable from the organisational and cultural and the latter is shaped by the organisational structures and principles of governance. Appropriate structures and governance of institutions are basically guided by the ethos and the academic traditions prevalent in a society.

In the other regions of distance-open education, different organisational structures and institutional cultures exist. Generally the organisational structures of institutions in the developing countries reflect hierarchical models and the cultures too become more-persons' centered than institutions centered. A typical organistaionl structure of a distance education institution in a developing country would be somewhat like this:

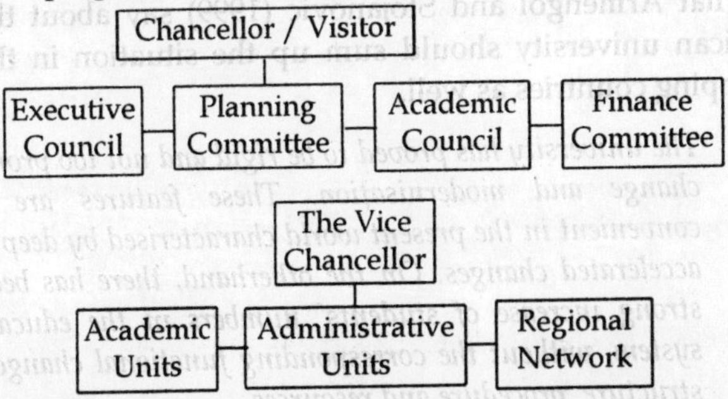

Figure 6 : *Organisational Structure of a Typical Distance Education Institution in a Developing Country*

For all day-to-day functions, the Vice-Chancellor has to function as a head supervisor, although a number of academic, administrative and regional services units have their normal functional heads. The statutory bodies such as the Executive Council/Board of Management etc. have representatives from the institutions concerned. But the agenda for the statutory bodies are usually prepared by the Vice-Chancellor or with his permission they get included. The meetings of the statutory bodies are chaired by the Vice-Chancellor and very rarely the Vice-Chancellor's proposals are turned down by he statutory bodies.

Within the institutions, the culture of the developing world is still hierarchical. Although formal democratic rights are granted in the statutes and the ordinances of the institutions, it is the top management which usually decides the merit of an issue—controversial or otherwise. Lobbies and powerful groups with vested interest do exist and they can influence the top management to take decisions in a manner acceptable to them, even if the decisions do not conform straightforwardly to the stated policies and norms of the institution. Democracy, thus, gets interpreted by the interest of power cliques rather than the interests of the institutions or the students. The inevitable fall out of such practices is that there always exists a kind of mistrust between the top management and the bulk of the staff. This mistrust has serious implications for the work culture at the institutions concerned.

What Armengol and Stojanovic (1999) say about the Latin American university should sum up the situation in the other developing countries as well.

> *The university has proved to be rigid and not too prone to change and modernisation. These features are not convenient in the present world characterised by deep and accelerated changes. On the otherhand, there has been a strong increase of students' numbers in the education system, without the corresponding functional changes of structure, procedure and resources.*

The structures and governance of distance teaching universities are still in the process of evolution. For understandable reasons, no distance teaching institution would like to deviate radically from the available models. It is common knowledge that successful model would always be useful to start with. But as the institutions grow in size and operations they must review and reflect on their practices. Wherever the structures prove to be hurdles, the institutions must develop sufficient confidence and flexibility to discard the useless structures and formalities and go for new appropriate structures and strategies. If the institutions fail to do that, they may have to pay dearly in terms of work efficiency and quality.

References

Armengol, M.C and Stojanovic, L (1999) "Distance Education : A Decision Force for the Latin American University" file:/C:/CDE. papers/35-Cas as Armengol.htm

Bittar, Ramona Akl (1999), "Latin American Distance Education Universities: Research For the Future", file://C:/DE-Papers/32-AKL Bitter.htm

Costello, Neil (1993), "Organisational cultures and distance learning" *Open Learning.*, June 1992.

Daniel John (1999) "Distance Learning in the Era of Networks : What are the Key Technologies?", Pan Commonwealth Forum : Empowerment through knowledge and Technology, Brunei Darussalam, 1-5 March 1999.

Deshpande, P.M. (1992) "Yashwantrao Chavan Maharastra Open University", *Indian Journal of Open Learning* (IJOL), Vol.1, No.1, pp.5-10.

Jose Chander, N. (1991), *Management of Distance Education*, Sterling publishers, New Delhi

Perry, Wlter (1987), Open University: A personal Account of the First Vice-Chancellor. The Open University Press, Milton Keynes, The United Kingdom, pp. 22, 213; 215

Prasad, V.S. (1992), "Dr. B.R. Ambedkar Open University : A Decennail Perspective", *Indian Journal of Open Learning*, Vol.1, No.2, pp.11-18.

Ram Reddy, G. (1986) *Ivory Towers Thrown Open*, Sterling Publishers, New Delhi.

5

Indira Gandhi National Open University and Distance Education in India —an Appraisal

Commenting on the pressure brought on the higher education system in India, G. Parthasarathy observed:

> *In a situation of this type, where the expansion of enrolments in higher education has to continue at a terrific pace and where available resources in terms of men and money are limited, the obvious solution, if proper standards are to be maintained and the demand for the higher education from different sections of the people is to be met, is to adopt the Open University System with its provision of higher education on part-time or own time basis. The Group, therefore, recommends that the Government of India should establish, as early as possible, a National Open University by an act of Parliament. (G. Parthasarathy, Report of the Working Group, 1974.)*

Rationale and Justification for a National Open University

The Report of the Working Group (1974) which justified the establishment of a National Open University identified a number of weaknesses in the correspondence education in India since 1962 and to overcome those very weaknesses, the group suggested the following to be the focal points in establishing the open university system in the country :

(a) The most crucial input, on which everything else would largely depend, is the preparation of proper reading material. While the contribution of audio-visual aids is not being denied, the written word continues to be the most potent instrument of education... it is, therefore recommended that the single most important step in setting up an open university in India should be the development of self-instructional materials which should be innovative on the one hand, and on the other hand, should be written with a view to meeting the requirements of students...

(b) Following upon the above, it is necessary to set up a core group of about a dozen scholars of merit not only in the selected field of scholarship, but also in that of preparing reading material suitable for different levels of educational endeavour which would be covered in the early stages of the open university; (Emphasis added).

(c) In the light of the insurmountable difficulties involved in making audio-visual aids and other infrastructure facilities available to each student individually, it is suggested that a study centre be set up for every 700 students or so where tapes, records, library facilities and faculty guidance should be made available to students of that area....

(d) To start with, it is suggested that the open university may set up not less than 8 centres to enroll about 5000 students...

(e) While the vehicle of the circular programmes of the university will be the reading material sent by post, broadcasts and telecasts, and the role of the teacher cannot be completely alienated some form of live contact with teachers will be a necessity.

(f) The organisation of the open university should be located in the Union Territory of Delhi and it should work in close collaboration with the universities and institutions of higher learning already in existence. This would have the obvious advantage of avoiding the creation of library and other facilities separately for the open university.

The Report of the working group had to wait for another 10 years to be acted upon. When the Indira Gandhi National Open University was established in 1985 September, the mandate given to it was broad and complex.

The broad aims of the IGNOU were stated as follows:

> *The university shall endeavour through education, research, training and extension to play a positive role in the development of the country, and based on the rich heritage of the country, to promote and advance the culture of the people of India and its human resources (INGOU Act 1985.)*

Among its specific aims, a number of challenges got included. The university was expected to:

> *"Strengthen and divercify the degree, certificate and diploma courses related to the needs of employment and necessary for building the economy of the country" and*

> *"provide access to higher education for large segments of the population and in particular the disadvantaged groups such as those living in remote and rural areas including working people, housewives and other adults who wish to upgrade or acquire knowledge through studies in various fields" (IGNOU Act 1985)*

In the area of coordination and determination of standards of distance education, the IGNOU was expected to design, develop and deliver its courses with a view to overcoming or rectifying the following weaknesses of the correspondence education identified by various studies (Vijaya Mullay, 1986; Reddy, 1986; Gupta, 1982):

(a) Most of the correspondence institutes do not have competent and adequate staff. The best teachers are not posted at these institutes. As a result, they have low motivation.

(b) More than one university in a State, having correspondence courses, means duplication of efforts, resulting in low enrolments in many places.

(c) Lessons are prepared in a hurry with no regards to quality.

(d) Not much attention is paid to the assignments; they are not evaluated, corrected and returned to the students in time.

(e) Most of the correspondence courses do not have 'study centres' and personal contact programmes are organised by only a few institutions.

(f) Too much reliance is placed on the printed material and latest communication technology is hardly used.

(g) There is considerable delay in the despatch of lessons of the students.

(h) Bodies charged with the running of these institutions are not organised properly.

(i) The system has the same rigidities in the courses offered as the formal system; the students offer the same courses and appear for the same examinations as the regular students.

(j) Laboratory and library facilities are rarely provided and where they exist they are much below the desired standard.

(k) They do not have an identity of their own as they work within the university structure. The latter pay perfunctory attention to the former.

(l) Efforts to evaluate and check the standards of these correspondence courses are rare. Therefore, their growth and working is haphazard, leaving much to be desired.

In order to rectify the above weakness, the following strategies were to be adopted by IGNOU:

- The Courses offered by IGNOU will be structured on modular pattern with the facility for accumulation of credits. Provision will be made for transfer of credits from the formal to the non-formal system, and vice-versa. The UGC and the Open University will frame detailed guidelines in this respect.
- The standards will be prescribed to determine the minimum level of learning at every stage of education, and criteria will be evolved to objectively asses this level

of attainment so that opportunities can be provided to all, be it housewives, agricultural or industrial workers and professionals to continue with their education.

- To strengthen the delivery system of the open university and the media support to its programmes, discussion will be held with the ministry of Information and Broadcasting for provision of separate radio and TV channels.
- In the discharge of its responsibility to coordinate the distance learning system and determine its standards, the National Open University will frame necessary statutes for the guidance/compliance of the State Governments that wish to establish their own open universities or want to take advantage of the facilities offered by the National Open University.
- Arrangements will be made to develop a network of courses in the open university system. This would mean that a student joining one open university can take courses from another open university. The system will, therefore, offer wide variety of academic programmes.
- It is essential that the quality of the open university programmes and the delivery system are ensured. Since adequate expertise and trained manpower in this area are limited, it will be necessary that the open universities develop programmes in close collaboration with the IGNOU. Further, the programme of action of the national policy on education highlighted the use of distance education in the process of encouraging in-service teacher education programmes, continuing education and the training of management personnel of the education system. Moreover, with a view to encourage media and technology in education system, the programme of action insisted on:
- Establishment of radio stations in teaching universities/colleges during the Seventh Plan:
- Provision of TV Channel by 1991-92.
- Creation of dedicated satellite system for education needs in the long run.

The justification for a National Open University was, therefore, genuine, and the expectations of it were also justified, given the educational scenario of the country and the potential of the open/distance education as evidenced by its practice elsewhere. But how successful has IGNOU been in its mission? To what extent has the National Open University succeeded in overcoming the weakness of correspondence education system? In what manner will it influence the open learning system in India, and possibly in the developing world? These questions need careful examination. The extensive quotes from the report of the Working Group (1974) and the IGNOU Act (1985) would suggest the parameters within which these questions could be examined.

The Model for the National Open University

Indira Gandhi National Open University (IGNOU) has been broadly modeled after the Open University, located in Miltonkeynes, the U.K. The British Open University, of course, has been the source of inspiration for almost all the committees, working groups, policy making bodies and individuals who have shaped the proposals for the development of the open university system in India. Had the inspiration been of the right kind, then the architects of IGNOU would have given more attention to the working mechanisms suitable to the country with many peculiarities and complexities and would have shown more caution in adopting the structural models of foreign open universities, especially the British Open University, than what they have done in these areas. While acknowledging the contributions of all those who have taken part in establishing the National Open University, one should not, at the same time, be indifferent to the weaknesses and inadequacies of institutional models and the ways of adopting and adapting them.

The structure of IGNOU, however, is more of an imitation of the British Open university than an adapted indigenous model to meet the specific needs and demands of the Indian learners. The pattern of governance, the academic units in the form of Schools of Studies, the support Divisions, the administrative wings, the media unit called the Communication Division (now renamed as Electronic Media Production Centre (EMPC), the structure of the Regional Services, the multimedia approach to teaching-learning and many other aspects of the university encompassing its structural features and policy considerations reflect the external features of the British Open University's structures and practices. However, the IGNOU structures and policies do not adopt any of those of the British Open University (BOU) in their entirety. The reasons for this have to be sought in the broader national context.

Because of the tendency to imitate others and go for convenient, and easy options the Indian planners usually end up with adhoc decisions (which suit the convenience of those who are at the helm of affairs). These adhoc decisions are justified in the name of flexibility and realism, whereas the simple truth is that well defined policies and principles are seldom aimed at with any sincerity at any stage. As a result, whenever there is a change in the top management, the entire institutional structure gets a jolt and often individual perceptions take the form of policy changes with little reference to the merits and demerits of the previous ones. To put it more concretely, whenever a new Vice-Chancellor is appointed to an Indian University, institutions are compelled to change their programmes or policies to satisfy the aspirations of the Vice-Chancellor or the priorities of powerful individuals which need not always be academically correct in achieving the institutional goals. As a matter of fact, institutional goals, in the form of precise mission statements, are seldom spelt out by Indian universities. This is true of IGNOU and many other universities established in recent times in India. Let us examine how.

If we analyse the portions of the IGNOU Act (1985) dealing with the goals of the National Open University, at least the following four major goals are spelt out.

- Democratisation of higher education in the country
- Promotion of education, training, research and extension activities based on the rich cultural heritage of the country
- Promotion of education of the disadvantaged groups of the population; and

- Coordination and determination of standards and quality of distance education through establishment and strengthening of open university system in the country which would flourish through multi-media based self-instructional materials and adequate student support services.

(There are many minor goals set for the University which need not be enumerated here.)

Any one of the above will be daunting enough for any university. A combination of all the above would of course be a formidable challenge which could be met only with thorough planning, adequate resources (human and material), clear vision, and above all, a sincere, professional commitment. Absence of any of the prerequisites would cause tremendous strains, if not a disaster, to any project of national magnitute. This awareness was very much emphasised both within and outside the University when it started its activities practically in 1986. More importantly, the need to overcome the academic and operational weaknesses of the correspondence education was repeatedly given as the justification for the open university system, the promotion of which would presumebly ensure the standards and quality of an innovative mode of higher education. Has the promise become a reality, or are there gaps?

The Right Beginnings

When the IGNOU decided to offer its academic programmes from January 1987, it was expected that the National Open University would set the pace for all other distance teaching institutions as well as the conventional universities in offering need based, socially relevant programmes which would have a reasonably good demand in the job market and also contribute to the over all development of the nation in terms of economy, education and culture. With this broad aim in mind, two pilot programmes were launched by IGNOU in January 1987: Diploma in Distance Education and Diploma in Management. Both these programmes were decided on the basis of some preliminary surveys which indicated the need, relevance and demand for both.

Diploma in Distance Education was primarily meant for developing human resources to develop and manage the distance education system in the country. The weaknesses of the system, as we mentioned earlier, were partly if not mainly, because of the shortage of qualified people to handle the activities of distance teaching institutions in the country. Therefore the Diploma Programme in Distance Education aimed at training the teachers and other personnel who would be functioning at various levels in the evolving system of distance education. Obviously, it was meant to be a specialised, professional, full fledged training programme for a relatively small number of people. The qualifications for the would be participants were also set very high: A post-graduate degree of four years duration at college level. The duration of the Diploma was one academic year and the maximum period allowed to complete the programme was four years. The first batch of 1100 students were admitted for this progoramme and their academic year started in January 1987.

The Diploma in Management, on the other hand, was meant to be a job oriented programme mainly for the working managers with limited professionalism. Since there existed a demand for management personnel, it was decided to supply the required numbers of professionally qualified managerial staff to various organisations. Two streams of students were admitted to this Diploma:

(a) those who had a graduation and three years of supervisory experience and

(b) those who did not have a graduation but who had six years of supervisory experience.

In 1987, about 4000 students were admitted to this programme.

Both the above programmes were meant to be pilot programmes. The aim was to test, study, and evaluate every aspect of the design, development and implementation of the two programmes offered through distance mode. Special attention was given to the self instructional features of the learning materials and the multi-media components which were expected to remove the weaknesses of the hitherto existing correspondence education programmes and thus, herald a new era in offering education through multimedia distance education.

The development of self-instructional materials (SIMs) in print as well as the audio-visual media was, in itself, an experiment. This was also necessary to carry out the major recommendation by the Parthasarathy Committee for the National Open University. Since there was no previous experience available in the country to develop self-instructional materials, a small group of 3 or 4 people headed by a senior academic undertook the task of developing the instructional material for the Distance Education Programme. The content, the design and the presentation were the main academic challenges to be met by the group. Though there were a few 'big names' in the country in the field of distance education recognised as 'experts', 'doyens', etc. they were of little help when it came to the actual task of systematically developing the self-instructional material for distance education.

Pressure of time and other constraints at this stage did not permit the idea of training the 3 or 4 junior academics for a reasonable period and then asking them to take up the task of developing the instructional materials. Therefore, the development of self-instructional materials, without any previous training or experience, except in the case of the senior academic, had to be accepted as a kind of on the job training. For the senior academics also, it was as much a training as it was a testing ground for him to give practical shape to his ideas and schemes. Mainly because of 'luck' in the form of 'freedom' to work, the experiment worked.

In a record time of six months, most of the self-instructional units/lessons in print were ready before the new additional staff joined in March-April 1987. The first dispatch of materials was sent to the students in January 1987 as scheduled. The intensity of work and the degree of commitment displayed by the small team of distance educators at the time could be understood only by those who had seen the day-to-day turn out of their intellectual production. The present day work culture obtaining in IGNOU would, of course, make it appear as a fairy tale!

Simultaneously, the team worked on audio-video programmes and also in offering consultancy services to the management programme in the areas of educational technology (locally known as formatting and editing). The efforts of the team reached the culmination in the successful despatch of the reading materials to the students, along with the programme guides and assignments. The audio-video programmes, though technically were produced by the media producers, the academic contribution to the development of the programmes had to come from the academics at every stage. The videos and audio's produced in the first half of 1987 were the outcome of absolutely untested methods and adventures of educational media production at the University. They were produced under the same pressure of time as the materials in print. In all fairness, the comitment of the media staff at the time was also to be treated as total, despite their limited experience with educational media production.

In the area of physical production of the materials in the form of booklets was another new experience. The printers identified for doing the job did not have much experience in bringing out the self-instructional material. Nor was it easy to convince them about the size of the pages, the booklets and the font size. The value of illustrations was not adequately appreciated by the semi-professional printers and commercial artists. There was an obvious gap between the academic need and the actual reproduction of illustrations in the print materials. There were also instances of mess up of tables, figures and diagrams at the final stages of production which upset the academics, especially after having repeatedly instructed the printers on the placement, design etc. of these. In the initial stage of production, some of the course materials had to be proofread eight or nine times by the academics because of the low professionalism of the composers and printers. Even in 1986 and 1987, only the age old type writers were used to prepare the manuscripts and it took a few more years for the university to get word processors and laser printers to prepare camera ready copies(CRCs) in-house. Inspite of the care taken, the printed booklets were not free from the 'printer's devils'. And so, the academics had to prepare the corrigenda for those booklets (Blocks) which had serious errors.

Those were the days when the handful of IGNOU academics had not known Saturdays and Sundays or holidays. They were not even aware of the benefits and losses of their career and occupational hazards. They had been gripped by some kind of commitment and a desire to do something in the field of education which had not been tried till then in India. This spirit and the missionary zeal were primarily responsible for the initial success of the two programmes which got the name and fame for the university. It was different matter that after having put the academic programmes very effectively on the map of educational innovations and reforms of India, those very academics both at the senior and junior levels, found themselves as unwanted or uncared for antiques in some corners of the university. New forces, which usually did not know about the national role of the university began to dominate the policy formulation and the decision making processes of the University. Instead of taking some necessary lessons from the pilot programmes, the university treated them as unquestionable success and therefore as the IGNOU Models for every academic programme of the University. And the future programmes, sadly enough, did not even follow the rigour of the pilot programmes when they were designed, developed and produced. The consequences of such casual treatment of distance teaching programmes were far reaching, and they are being felt now after 14-15 years, not so much by the University administration and the academia as by the students of the university. If the performance of the courses and the other aspects of programme evaluation are taken up seriously, the magnitude of the problems faced by students could be measured in full measure.

The Pilot Programmes and the Aftermath

The pilot programmes were, in a sense, gradually treated as the models by those who did not have much understanding about the open learning system. Some of the physical features such as the format of the self-instructional course units, audio-video cassettes, counselling-cum-contact sessions for the students at the study centres, assignments, continuos assesments, term-end-examinations, etc, were merely copied by the various Schools of Studies of the University, without realising and internalising the underlying philosophies of each of the external features of open learning through distance mode. Questions like

> '*How many sections should a unit have?*'
>
> '*How many sub-sections and self-check exercises per section or a unit?*'
>
> '*How many units should a course have?*'
>
> '*How many audio videos per course?*'

etc. were repeatedly asked and got answered, more as rules of thumb than as the genuine academics needs of courses or programmes. These continued and still continue as questions for debate even after the academics are being told repeatedly that such questions do not get real answers from the official/administrative decisions, though for practical purposes the University could fix a limit on the number of audio-videos for example mainly from the monetary considerations. The implicit answer is that the above questions need to be answered by those very academics who raise them in an academic way and not to wait for the official green signals, at least in matters where money is not involved. But this basic academic right does not seem to have been understood by the academic community even today. Unless there is external pressure, particularly from learners, this academic right may not be exercised at all.

Environmental Weaknesses of Indian Universities vis-a-vis IGNOU

The tension between the academic community and the management of the university is obvious. What is not obvious is the tension between the learners on one hand and the support they are promised by the university on the other. The reasons for the perpetual adhocism leading to the inevitable tension at the National Open University have to be traced to some of the crucial decisions taken at the very early stages of the evolution of the University. Although a bill was passed in the Parliament with high hopes to usher in a new era of educational changes, especially at the higher level, with the necessary political will to back up the project, something in the academic environment and the intellectual level has been missing at the University from its inception. The autonomy given to the university was and has been interpreted and reinterpreted everytime by the political bosses, government functionaries, the senior officers and the bureaucrats of the University at every level. The University academic community as such had little freedom and less competence, at least initially in deciding its policies, although on paper, it was supposed to enjoy complete freedom to function within the frame-work of the Act and the statutes of the University. Again, the statutes were so prepared that any number of interpretations and meanings could be given by the groups within the statutory bodies of the University to influence the decisions in a particular way. This need not necessarily be the unique privilege of the National Open University.

In simple terms, the political pressures would compel the Vice-Chancellor of any Indian University to find ways to accommodate demands which in the normal circumstances a Vice-Chancellor could turn down unhesitatingly. But in a socio-political environment which accords neither the status nor the powers of a vice-chancellor of a reputed western university, it would be unrealistic to expect any Indian Vie-Chancellor to act in an academic way and still remain in his post. Usually a delicate balance is maintained by the Vice-Chancellor between the interests of the university on the one hand and the political interest of the government on the other. To do so even, the Vice-Chancellor must have some academic status, will power, perseverance, integrity and enormous patience to persuade the bureaucrats who usually cannot be persuaded to change their 'views' on any thing under the sun. If the Vice-chancellor is weak in all these attributes, which is the case in many Indian Vice-Chancellors, then a university will become another political stage to carry out the hidden agenda of the unenlightened politicians vested with the powers to decide the educational policies of the country. Usually power triumphs over pedagogy, often with the willingness of the latter to submit.

Because of this unenviable situation, the statutory bodies of the Indian universities remain either as ineffective, nominal mechanisms or as the tools in the hands of the government or the 'powerful' Vice-Chancellors. The very composition of the statutory bodies would tell us that these bodies cannot usually ensure the autonomy of the universities. As a rule, the statutory bodies are dominated by the government representatives and their nominees. Some 'powerful' members of the statutory bodies such as the Education Secretary and the Finance Secretary can easily brush aside the views of the rest of the members, including the views of Vice-Chancellors, if they have to assert their positions as Secretaries. If the Vice-Chacellors are weak and if the other members of the statutory bodies are obliged to the government functionaries, then, whatever little autonomy that could be exercised by the universities will be mortgaged. There is yet another situation. When the majority of the members are new to the system, in this case, the open learning system, they are bound to be influenced by the conventional education system, its requirements, norms, traditions, standards and practices. In that case, pushing in any new concept or scheme to be experimented would be extremely difficult. However, the National Open University and its Vice-Chancellors have so far been lucky in getting the support of the state and its functionaries in most cases. What, then, could be the factors which may affect the University adversely?

Special Requirements of an Open University

Granting that none of the above mentioned negative factors become obstructions in a given situation and the university is given 'complete' academic freedom to decide its policies, design its programmes/courses and implement them in the best possible manner, there still remain the questions of acquiring the knowledge, expertise and commitment to do so. The basic attributes of an academic institution are the ability

(a) to attract the best academic talents,

(b) to create an atmosphere to generate adventure of ideas and spirit of enquiry, and

(c) inspire the trust and the willingness of the academic community to share its knowledge and experience with the rest of the society.

These attributes are customary to conventional universities in that generation of knowledge, preservation of knowledge and extension of knowledge are traditionally encouraged through teaching, research and extension activities. In open university system these attributes become imperative for the very existence of the system. In the practice of these principles, the open universities need, first and foremost, a community of teachers, scholars or academics who have the necessary knowledge and expertise of required standards and quality.

In the conventional universities, centuries old traditions and norms exist for selection of the best minds suitable to perform their functions. For the open universities no such traditions exist, and the traditions, if at all they are established, get transformed frequently because of the unconventional roles and functions assigned to the open universities as well as the academics and other functionaries. The traditional concept of teaching and research undergoes a sea change because of the demands made on the teachers by the requirements of the open learning system. The principal difference between a teacher of traditional university and a teacher of an open university is the role assigned to each. The conventional university teacher is a master of his own activities. The only restrictive domains are the prescribed syllabi and the number of hours for teaching in the class room. He/She is an individual teacher with his/her personality traits, attributes, ideas, beliefs, values, ideology etc. It is this individual identity that becomes paramount for a conventional teacher.

In the distance-open-university system, although a teacher is expected to have outstanding academics qualifications on par with his traditional counterpart, he, in many ways loses his individual identity, since he is seen as a team member. He becomes a partner in a collective activity: teaching through distance mode. Not-withstanding the impact of new technology and media, this basic distinction of roles keeps apart a distance teacher and a classroom teacher.

This change of role, along with a change of functions, and identity generates tension, at least in the beginning, among the open university teachers and others who are collectively engaged in the design, development and implementation of the curricula and programmes of the distance-open learning system. This crucial difference in the role, identity and functions of teachers between the two systems of education must be recognised at the very beginning of the open university activities in any country which goes for such an experiment for the first time. If the requirements of a new system are not properly understood and appreciated by the policy making bodies and the academic community of an open university at the initial stage, innumerable contradictions would develop in the years to come and the problems and tensions caused by those contradictions cannot be easily resolved.

Precisely because of some appreciation for, and knowledge about these contradictions, problems and tensions to be anticipated, the IGNOU pilot programmes were launched in 1987 with a view to ascertaining the requirements of the university and the course it should chart for itself in the following terms:

- The need(s) for a particular programme to be launched by an open university
- Demand(s) for certain other programmes which sell well in the employment market
- Appropriate curricula for the open university system
- Effective strategies to design, develop and implement the programmes
- Ways to study the heterogeneity of learners and their profile
- Ways and means to meet the diverse needs of the open university learners
- Adequacy and the preparedness of the University in the meeting the challenges in terms of resources, infrastructure and efficiency, if not experience which in any case was limited
- Potential and the attitude of the staff in carrying out their tasks

- Requirements of staff development
- Efficacy and feasibility of student support services put into practice
- Effectiveness and performance of the multimedia packages prepared for the two pilot programmes and their implications for the future programmes of the University; and
- The experience gained through the two pilot programmes based on which the entire system of distance education would evolve and grow in the years to come.

An Opportunity Lost. And Lost Forever?

In short, the pilot programmes were meant to be experiments to be studied by the University which was new in its operations of the kind which demanded, not only sound theoretical knowledge about distance-open learning programmes but also rich experience in handling them at every stage. Since the University was quite unsure about the strategies to be followed in translating the theoretical understanding of the few senior level academics into practice, it wanted to carefully document, study and evaluate every move of those who had the responsibility to design, develop and implement the pilot programmes. A thorough evaluation of every aspect of the two pilot programmes was appreciated at all levels within the University, at least in theory, because such an evaluation was perceived as the corner-stone for its future expansion in every respect: the number of progrmmes and courses, students enrollment, staff recruitment and staff training, research in the context of an open university, the strategies to be followed in the preparation of multimedia packages, the type of student support services, the forms of student evaluation, programme evaluation and the whole range of activities related to the operational schedules of the university such as the admissions, printing/production of course materials, dispatch of materials, handling of assignment responses and their movement, conduct of academic counselling sessions, handling students' problems, conduct of examinations etc. and the cost factor involved in all these. In simple terms, the evaluation of the pilot programmes would have given the necessary feedback to the university to ascertain whether the university was proceeding along the right course.

The evaluation of the two pilot programmes, however, was never attempted. Even before the pilot programmes had their first run, something very different happened. A decision was taken to launch the Bachelors' Degree Programme (BDP) in the three traditional academic areas: social sciences, humanities and sciences. Schools of studies consisting of traditional disciplines suddenly sprang up. Academic staff, media staff, administrative staff and the support staff were recruited on a massive scale.

The 'Big Bang' and the Fallout

The Bachelor's Degree Programme (BDP) struck the University unexpectedly with a devastating force. If one were to write the early history of IGNOU in its first decade, one would have little hesitation in viewing the launching of the BDP as the single most unfortunate decision made by the University, not so much because of the relevance of the programme in an open university but because of the suddenness and the manner in which it was launched. The cautious and hesitant moves of the University in experimenting and evolving a nucleus around which the entire future system of distance-open learning was expected to develop and grow were completely thrown out of gear through the launching of BDP. The focus of the University suddenly shifted from evolving a new system to legitimising the accommodation of courses, policies, practices and thinking of a conventional variety. Instead of training and reorienting the traditional academics to contribute effectively to the functioning and growth of the new system, the system was compelled to slow down its process of system building and respond to the needs of the conservative, traditional and non-committal tendencies of those guided by the spirit and attitude of college teachers in small towns, affliated to and afflicting Indian universities usually functioning as examining bodies rather than to act as centres of excellence in the generation of knowledge and its preservation and extension. Instead of offering an appropriate place and space for traditional academic programmes in an open university, the BDP was accorded, unwittingly though, a special and central place which in effect became a trap for the entire University. Academic disciplines themselves do not become indepediments to open universities but the traditional attitudes of the academics who teach them do.

The relevance of humanities, social sciences and sciences in a university, whether open or traditional, is never in dispute. But the place and importance given to them and the strategies to impart the different sub-disciplines covered by them are always matters of great concern. The continuity of the humanist and liberal education demands that the above mentioned three academic areas should never be given up for the reasons of economic pragmatism. The exigencies of market forces always focus on the demand, rather than the needs of the social units. Liberal arts, social sciences and humanities have significance in that they have power to raise the basic questions about the social movements, the relationship between the individual and the society as also between the institutions, the goal of human endeavour, the aesthetic aspects of human life and so on. Natural sciences have the same relevance, so far as their ability to develop scientific temper and spirit of enquiry in students goes. These disciplines become all the more important in the context of a consumerist society based on individualism, commercialism and cash nexus, in order to retain some of the human values.

But the real question for an open university is not that of the relevance of the traditional academic disciplines but one of deciding the space for them and the strategies to offer them. Having accepted the importance of these disciplines in the social context, an open university must also consider their place in the overall aims and objectives of the institution. From the stand point of the objectives, traditional academic programmes should find a relatively limited space in the University's list of activities. But the reality was and still is exactly the opposite. The three major schools of studies—the School of Social Sciences, the School of Humanities and the School of Sciences—became the most visible academic units of the university, besides the School of Management Studies.

The large scale recruitment of teaching and non-teaching staff of the major Schools of Studies obviously changed the staff profile and the academic thinking of the university.

The sheer number of academics coming from the traditional stream of classroom teaching or with no teaching experience at all made a difference in shaping the attitudes of the staff towards distance-teaching open-learning system as a whole. The newly appointed staff had neither the previous experience in the distance teaching system, nor the time to reorient themselves to effectively contribute to the new mode of teaching-learning. They needed time to assimilate the limited training programmes arranged for them at the university but they were called upon to perform all the tasks of distance educators. There was no mechanism to monitor the impact of the training programmes on the teaching staff or on the institutional policy to evaluate the quality of the study materials developed by them. Too many activities were taken up too suddenly with too little preparation. The hurried nature of all these actions has had its effect on the learning effectiveness of the materials developed by the academic staff in that the learners, particularly of BDP, find it extremely difficult to meet the demands of the programmes. The pass rate of BDP would further testify this claim.

The experience otherwise gained through the two pilot programmes should have been used substantially. The informal feedback on the implementation of the two programmes was shared rather informally by the staff, but there was no conscious attempt on the part of the University to pass any legislation on the quality of teaching-learning and the academic credibility of courses. From the beginning, there was a certain casualness about the development and delivery of the programmes of the University. Very often the approaches to course development both in print and the electronic media were decided by some dominant individuals, who were not necessarily the experts, notwithstanding the names given on the credit pages of the blocks.

'Academic freedom' and 'autonomy' were interpreted in many different ways by the academics themselves, depending on their understanding or lack of it with regard to preparation of course materials, choice of media, student support services, evaluation procedures, etc. On the other hand, academics did not have any autonomy in deciding the schedules and the processes of programme preparation and delivery. Because it was the beginning stage of the University, there was little time for academic debates and discussions on the methodological issues, and the same reason was enough to exercise a kind of bureaucratic control over the academic activities which otherwise would have become intellectually challenging, creative and rewarding. As a result, there developed a situation where everyone felt that he/she was right and others were wrong. And the senior managers of the University felt that the academics were fussy about everything and were eager to find excuses to avoid the work. It was a typical situation of the academics versus the administrators/ authorities in any open university in the early stages.

Besides the above mentioned conflicts, there were other problems too. The various Schools and Divisions were functioning from various buildings in the different parts of Delhi. Communication and coordination among the units became difficult, especially when schedules had to be met. The other infrastructural facilities such as office accommodation, electricity, water supply, transport etc. were poor, affecting the working conditions adversely. All these had implications for the overall efficiency of work, its quality and the attitude of the staff towards the system as such. The general impression among the staff was that there was too much of imposition on them from the top management and too little freedom for the academics to think and do in the teaching-learning process. Because of perceptions such as these, there was a general resistance from the academics to any attempt to orient them to the open learning system. The attempted 'conversion' was naturally viewed by the academics as 'brain washing' or 'indoctrination'.

Preparation of Study Materials—Problem Areas

Although IGNOU has expanded its activities tremendously, the management of these activities remain a daunting task. Right from the planning stage up to the implementation and evaluation of the academic programmes of the University, there are a number of challenges which need to be met in a professional way. Planning of academic programmes has to take into account a series of steps such as : the potential learner groups, the needs of the learners, their socio-academic background, their geographical location (urban, rural, remote areas), the previous knowledge of students, the minimum requirements to cope with the programme, the appropriate curriculum and syllabus, the students' workload, the appropriate media policy in relation to student support services, monitoring mechanism, evaluation scheme, provision for review and evaluation and the factors affecting all these. Some of these are taken care of as official requirements, but not as professional imperatives of the system.

Quite often decisions regarding the choice of programmes are taken intuitively or on the basis of suggestions and recommendations by experts and academics in the relevant disciplines. Broad proposals containing some information on the need or demand for the programmes, potential target groups and their number, the job prospects of those who complete the programmes, the content areas, mode of delivery, medium of instruction, approximate cost involved, the evaluation scheme and the schedule for launching the programmes are prepared by the faculty. These proposals are later discussed and approved with the necessary changes by the respective School Boards, the Planning Board, the Academics Council and the Board of Management. Once the formal approval is obtained from the statutory bodies of the University, the faculty concerned start working on the development of programmes.

A programme is the superordinate term which includes in it a few courses. A course will have a few booklets called blocks and each block will have 3 or 4 self-instructional units/lessons. The development of courses goes through a lengthy process—experts committee meeting to design the curricula and the syllabi, course writers' meetings to distribute the units to be written followed by a short orientation programme to orient/train the writers to write units as per the requirements of programme/courses, involvement of the audio-video producers, content and linguistic editing by experts, formatting and redesigning of the units by educational technologists, printing and proof reading and the entire process of physical production of the course materials. After the preparation of study materials, major challenges have to be met while implementing the programmes. But academics have little control over the strategies of operations and implementation, which is a different story.

Explorations in the Unfamiliar Areas

The process of course development itself is quite complex and cumbersome. The major difficulty is to identify the right kind of course writers and decide upon the approach to course development. In India, it is easy to get a large number of good classroom teachers who are knowledgeable, communicative and successful in their profession. But it is difficult to get them to write for distance learners. Writing for different levels of distance learners requires special skills and expertise which were be clearly recognised by the Working Group when it emphasised the need to set up a core group of about a dozen scholars of merit in the selected disciplines who would also have expertise to prepare appropriate reading materials suitable for different levels of programmes/courses to be offered by the National Open University.

The National Open University found it difficult to attract the minimum required number of scholars of merit, let alone the scholars of merit with the additional necessary expertise to design and develop the appropriate study materials in the selected disciplines and at different levels. Since this basic academic requirement is yet to be fully met, IGNOU has been facing time and again the same problem of assured professionalism. From the very beginning of the University's activities, the priority has been to meet the compulsive schedules—schedules to prepare the materials, schedules to launch the programmes, schedules for counselling sessions and examinations and so on, without having created a knowledge base to fullfil the schedules to launch the progrmmes, schedules for counselling sessions and examinations and so on, in a professional way. This weakness in creating a strong academic nucleus forewarns far reaching consequences for the character and inner functioning of the university. The positive image about the university in the public is simultaneously challenged by the numerous complaints from the students about the delays and distortions of operations and functions mainly because of inappropriate logistics. Many of the academic achievements get overshadowed or distracted by operational and administrative weaknesses.

In the academic domain, the poverty of scholarship and paucity of distance teaching experience effectively contribute to the fixing of unrealistic schedules, and selection of untested, ill-equipped course writers, and other personnel who cannot meet the challenges of distance open learning. As a result, the content and the presentation of self-instructional units neatly packed inside the uniform format accepted by the University may not meet the objectives set for the programmes/courses. As a result, students in some major programmes like the BDP face many difficulties. Younger academics had to correct many distortions of draft units, when detected, but the impact of the unprofessional approach course development cannot be wished away. The impact of inadequate planning, casual approach to professional issues and their clumsy execution should be seen in the actual performances of courses/programmes, even if the learning materials could be accepted generally as of high quality. Senior academics and officers of the university need to play their roles to improve the present situation. They can play their roles effectively, only if they could take staff development and systemic research seriously.

Audio-Video Programmes

Preparations of print materials appeared to be an easy job, if one had looked at the development of audio-video materials meant to be complementary or supplementary to the materials in print in those early days. Although the cost of development and production of audio-video materials was many times high, the University took a decision to produce audios and videos because it was thought that 'multi-media' distance education must have audio-video programmes without which the university could not get the status of a distance teaching open university. The fascination for the multimedia had to contend with its pedagogic value. The concept of multimedia approach to distance education was at time stretched to the extreme. If a course or a progrmme did not have a specific number of audios and videos, it ws considered to be a correspondence course/programme, and not one of distance education.

The meaning of multi-media is of course not restricted to print, audios and videos. The other media such as the telephone, telecast, broadcast, computer-tutoring, computer-assisted-learning, face-to-face contact-cum-counselling sessions etc. were unconsciously excluded from the multimedia territory. The common dictum that "any medium is as good and as effective as any other media" was never understood or noted. As a rule of thumb, every block (a booklet of 3-4 units of print-materials) was expected to have one video and two audios. In terms of content, it was agreed to give additional information through audios and videos on the themes discussed in the print materials. But what actually went into the audio-video programmes is a matter of opinion rather than a verified fact. The informal feedback from the academics of the University shows that most of the audio-video programmes have repeated the same information already available in the printed texts. Considering the comparative cost of the development of audio-video programmes and their actual use by the students, one gets the impression that academic use value of the electronic media is very marginal in the present circumstances. To justify the cost, the university needs to pay more attention to the access and the educational value of the multimedia. Focused research into these issues would provide valuable insights and the much needed direction for the media policy of the University.

The Problem of Access

Apart from the debatable quality of the audio-video programmes from the academic point of view, their access to IGNOU students is another prickly issue. Very few IGNOU students have the facility of owning their own VCPs and tape recorders. Most students have to go to the study centres of the University to use the audio-videos. The morning broadcast of

IGNOU programmes on the Doordarshan (Indian Television) is a welcome step to increase the access but?.... The Working Group (1974) actually recommended that there should be one study centre for 700 students which is a modest provision. Considering the difficulties of the students in visiting the study centres, the University has, in fact improved the physical provision of study centres by reducing the ratio. As per the present policy, 200 students will be attached to one study centre. Counselling-cum-tutoring is offered at the study centres along with the necessary infrastructure facilities to watch the videos and listen to the audios during or after the counselling sessions. At present, there are 380 study centers of IGNOU monitored by 42 Regional Centres located across the country. There are about 800 Co-ordinators, and Assistant Co-ordinators and 19,500 part-time Academic-counselors to facilitate, and assist the students in their learning. The physical arrangements for the student services look impressive indeed. However, there are constraints and practical difficulties in ensuring quality of services to the 7,00,000 students opting for 610 Courses.

Constraints such as the distance between the study centre and the living place of the student, time, monetary expenditure and, above all, the lack of psychological preparedness of the students do not encourage the students to visit the study centres regularly or often. Keeping in view these difficulties, the university has made the attendance at the study centres optional, except in the cases of practical/ laboratory sessions. The average attendance at an IGNOU study centre is below 20 percent, and there is no way of confirming whether the same set of students attend more than one counselling session. Access to study centres, thus, has implications for access to audio-video programmes as well as their actual use.

Attendance for the academic counselling sessions at the study centres of IGNOU would point to many inherent weaknesses of the student support system at the University. Lakshmi Reddy (1995), for instance, records varying ranges of attendance of students at the counselling sessions conducted by the university in the different regions of the country. The lowest percentage is 2.7 % and the highest percentage is 82.3 %. Reddy suggests the following as the possible reasons for the wide variations in attendance:

- The students might not have felt the need for counselling-cum-personal contact sessions.
- Delay in passing on the information about the counselling schedules to students might have discouraged them.
- Students might not have received the study materials in time and therefore were not ready for counselling.
- Students might not have got the time to attend the sessions.
- The distance, travel, cost etc. involved in attending the sessions may be prohibitive.
- Students might have thought the sessions as unrewarding.
- At times counsellors might not have turned up.
- The functioning of the study centres might have been unsatisfactory.
- Accommodation and the physical facilities for the students attending the sessions might have been poor.
- Frequent interruption of electricity supply might have disappointed the students coming to watch the videos and listen to the audios at the study centers.
- The option given to the students to stay away from the counselling sessions might have created in them a casual attitude towards the very concept of counseling.

One or all the above may be the reasons for the poor attendance at the counselling sessions held at the study centres of IGNOU. Whatever be the other reasons for the low turn out of students for counselling, the implication of this for the system of students support is clear enough. The design and the delivery of services may not be appropriate and they have to be reorganised thoughtfully. By doing so, the institution will demonstrate its strength to make use of the available resources economically and purposefully.

Roughly one third of IGNOU budget is spent on maintaining the 22 Regional centres, 380 Study centres, and a division called Regional Service Division located at the headquarters. Apart from the regular staff, the University has appointed 19,500 academics counselors, and 800 co-ordinators and assistant co-ordinators on part-time basis to assist the regular staff in the main to conduct face-to-face contact-cum-counselling sessions, and assess the assignment responses from the students. The regional centres are to guide and monitor the activities of the study centres besides liasing with the headquarters on various issues related to the student concerns and problems.

No authentic study is available to give reliable evidence to show that the regional centres and the study centres have been successful in achieving their intended goals, although impressive figures are available regarding the number of counselling sessions, etc. For instance, during the year 1995-96 alone 84000 counselling sessions were organised for IGNOU students who had registered for various programmes/courses. But how many sessions were devoted to each of the 435 courses? How many of the 3,20,000 students could attend and how many sessions? What was the quality of counselling offered? What was the feedback from the students? These are some of the mute questions for which there are no answers. Even for someone to conduct an independent study on these issues, there is no easy access to records of the university, and if at all the records are made available, the information is either inaccurate and unreliable or it is inconsistent. Despite the fact that the University is heavily computerised, there is no way of getting reliable information on the following simple matters:

- Numbers of students registered for a programme or a course year wise
- Number of students who have passed out in each batch programme wise/course wise and year wise
- Number of active and passive students (whatever be the definition of being 'active' and 'passive')—programmes wise, coursewise and yearwise.

Reliable and accurate information on the above would give us the true account of the performances of courses/programmes which in turn will help us assess the actual performance of the university in fulfilling its multiple roles as (a) an open university

(b) as the apex body for promotion, coordination and determination of standards of distance education in the country (c) as the national resource centre to support and promote distance education and (d) as centre of excellence in training in distance education for the promotion of distance education in India and abroad. An evaluation of all the major activities of the University would also inform us as to what extent the open university system has succeeded in over coming the shortcoming of the correspondence system of education.

Performance of Programmes/Courses

Performance of IGNOU programmes and courses would be a revealing factor in so far as the effectiveness and credibility of the distance/open learning system in India are concerned. The usual tendency of the votaries of distance-open learning, especially in the developing countries like India is to project the numbers—the counselling sessions, study centres, audio-video programmes etc.—to paint a rosy picture about the growth of the system. Expansion, of course, is an important indicator of the credibility of, or demand for the system. It is also a useful and necessary political banner to mobilise and sustain the open learning system which is relatively new to the learning culture of countries with strong oral traditions. However, mere expansion alone cannot mean growth, unless expansion is sustained through qualitatively high performance of courses and students.

The emphasis on the quality of performance is deliberate in the context of the establishment of IGNOU which has the responsibility to promote, coordinate and determine standards of distance education in India. By implication, the performance of IGNOU programmes, will also influence the University's international role and prestige particularly in the developing world.

How do the IGNOU programmes perform?

Since the information on the above is not readily available, one has to gather it mainly from the Convocation Reports and the Annual Reports of the University. The information thus gathered and compiled is presented in the following table.

Table : 1 Performance of IGNOU progrmmes: Number of students passed during the period 1987-1996.

Convocation Sl. No	Year	Total number of students passed out Out	Total number of students enrolled during the period 1987-1995 enrolled during the period	
1	1989	1,170	4,381	(1986-87)
2	1991	3,807	16,811	(1987-88)
3	1992	4,907	42,324	(1988-89)
4	1993	4,444	48,281	(1989-90)
5	1994	7,580	52,376	(1990-91)
6	1995	9,246	62,375	(1991-92)
7	1996	11,400	75,666	(1992-93)
			78,693	(1993-94)
			91,398	(1994-95)
		42,554	4,72,305	

Source: *Vice -chancellor's Reports to Convocations 1-7 and The Annual Reports for the period 1987-1995.*

The pass percentage works out to be roughly 11% which is quite low by any standards. The breakup of the number of students who have passed out programme wise/discipline wise would be very revealing. But the difficulty in accessing the relevant information in this regard does not permit a micro level analysis of that kind. However, some broad categorisation of progrmmes (area wise) and their performance would be indicative of the trends. Management programmes for example, dominate the University scenario whereas the Bachelors' Degree Programme which has enrolled the maximum number of students has shown a rather dismal performance. The Distance Education Programmes primarily meant for developing the human resources for the system of distance-open learning in the country show a reasonably good and consistent performance, though the intake for these programmes has to be necessarily limited. Of the 42,554 students graduated during the period 1989-1996, the breakup of some are shown in Table 2

Table 2: Number of students passed in some key areas of study during the period 1989-96.

Area(s) of Study	No. of students passed Out during the first Seven convocations	No. of students enrolled
Management Programme	30952	Not readily available
Distance Education Programme	1110	7468
Bachelors Degree Programme	1915	Not readily available
Others	8554	Not readily available
Total	42554	472305

Source: *Vice-Chancellor's Reports to Convocations 1-7 IGNOU.*

There are a number of difficulties in working out the pass percentage for the programmes and courses. The programmes allow the students varying durations for completing their studies. The norm is something like this: every Diploma programme offered by the University can be completed by the students in a minimum period of one year or a maximum period of four years. Bachelors' Degree can be obtained in a minimum period of three years and a maximum period of eight years. Because of this flexibility we cannot work out the exact pass percentage of a particular programme till it runs full cycle. However, where information is available on the programmes which have run for the maximum period allowed, it is possible to give the pass percentage and use them as the indicators. Looked at this way, we can talk about the performance of some of the programmes. But at the moment, even that is not possible because of lack of information.

A more detailed analysis of coursewise performance would reveal the actual performance of the programmes. For example, the 7th Convocation Report says that only 4 students graduated in the B.Sc. programme from among the 2000 odd students who registered in the first batch. The same report says that 800 students passed in the Bachelors' Degree Programme. The breakup is B.A.: 701; B.Com. : 175; B.Sc. : 4. B.A(701) is further divided into discipline based specialisation's, such as English (30), Hindi (19), History (33), Public Administration (39), Political Science (45), Sociology (42) and Economics (7), but the break up does not tally with the total number of B.A, Graduates. The actual number of BAs comes to 215 only. Further, the number of students passed in a discipline may belong to different batches/cohorts. For example, the 33 graduates in History may belong to any batch or batches registered between 1987 and 1993. So, the exact position of the given cohorts of a given discipline is not revealed by the general figures presented in the Convocation Reports or the Annual Reports. A more rigourous scrutiny is needed to arrive at exact figures on this count. This is possible, only when programme evaluation is taken up by every School and Discipline of the University. These are a few examples, not of wishful distortions but of unsystematic and casual approach to record keeping which is in need of improvement. The situation remains the same in 2001 also.

Needed — Proper Records of Students

Exact information on the performance of courses and programmes becomes important for other purposes as well. If the University has to succeed in offering 'individualised' instruction and need based, flexible academic programmes, then proper records of students must be meticulously maintained. To decide whether a student is active or passive or has dropped out, one has to look at the individual records of the students. At present, no such records are readily available for most programmes. On the other hand 3 full fledged support divisions exist in the University to do exactly this job: the Computer Division, Students Registration and Evaluation Division, and the Regional Services Division with its fleet of regional and study centres. Most complaints coming from students are about non-receipt of study materials, non-receipt of assignment responses, incorrectly recorded statements of grades/marks and so on, which could effectively be tackled if only the University has the expertise to build and maintain a database with the help of the abundantly available computer and other technologies.

For review purposes too, information about the performances of individual programmes/courses is vital. While calculating the cost of programmes, performance is an important factor because of the social aspect of the cost factor. Besides, the work and workload of the academics, academic policies, curricular, pedagogic and delivery issues etc. are determined on the basis of the performance and the future of the programmes. Professionalism demands that every aspect of a programme needs to be considered before a decision is taken regarding its creation, survival and withdrawal.. If the performance of a programme is ignored for any reason, then, the number of students registering for that programme every year will have little relevance in continuing that programme. Other aspects such as staff strucutre, additional staff positions, budgets to support services etc. will have to be considered from the performance angle. Of course, "performance" does not mean the completion rate alone. Peformance in the larger context would mean the social acceptability of a given programme as well. The students who earn their degrees, diplomas and certificates must get due recognition from the job market too. This is an important area of research where IGNOU could focus on. However, to do that, it is necessary to collect the relevant data on the completion rate for each programme/course. In the present era of Information Technology (IT) and computerisation, it should not be difficult for the university to meet the challenges it is faced with right now.

Conclusion

Indira Gandhi Open University (IGNOU) is one of the series of examples of educational institutions set up with noble aims which some how, have displayed a genius to create hurdles for themselves in achieving their goals. The enthusiasm and hope that marked the establishment of IGNOU in September 1985 by an act of the Indian Parliament was matched by the dedication and commitment of a handful of people who worked day and night to give a practical shape to the concept of a national open university in India. That commitment very soon gave way to clever diplomacy, showmanship, glamour, psychophancy, and all other kinds of unacademic tendencies. The expansion of IGNOU activities has made University vulnerable to many risks and instabilities both at the academic and the administrative fronts. As a result, the outwardly growth of IGNOU in terms of its size, number of programmes, courses, students, regional centres, study centres etc. is in sharp contrast to its fragile inner strength to sustain its wide range of activities in an efficient and professional way. Whether IGNOU will be able to fulfill its original mandate or will continue with policies and practices of adhocism and expediency which may act against the academic health of the university is the question the answer to which will decide the future of distance education in the country.

The Vice-Chancellor's report for the 10th Convocation of IGNOU (2001) mentions that the University at present has 62 programmes comprising 610 courses and an accumulated enrolment of over 700,000 students who are pursuing their different courses and programmes at different stages. This impressive expansion of the University has also to face major challenges in its administrative and student support systems without which quality assurance can not become a reality. Along with the growing number of courses and students the corresponding problems related to operational aspects should persuade the University to go for strict monitoring and evaluative mechanisms to help the University in rectifying minor problems quickly without allowing them to become major hurdles.

IGNOU is one of the 10 mega universities in the world—a mega university being one with more than 100,000 students on its rolls. It has a wide network and presence throughout the country. Some of its programmes such as PG Diploma and M.A in Distance Education, Management programmes and Computer Science progrmames have gained international recognition. Given a bold and imaginative initiative, IGNOU can emerge as a strong leader in distance education in the developing world. IGNOU's powerful Electronic Media Production Centre (EMPC) has tremendous potential to make the University's teaching—

learning process more interactive. The Staff Training and Research Institute of Distance Education (STRIDE) can fulfil its national and international obligations, provided it gets proper and the necessary institutional back up. The Distance Education Council (DEC) could act more efficiently as the apex body to coordinate and determine standards of distance education in the country, provided, again, it too gets the right kind of leadership and a strong academic dose in its staffing pattern. Many of the innovative programmes of the university in the fields of engineering and technology, nursing, local governance (Panchayathi Raj), construction, water management, disaster management, human rights, education of the disadvantaged groups, nutrition and child care, forest management, tourism, women's empowerment etc. have the potential to redefine the concept of a university of the 21st century India. But the potential, in order to become real, the University has to adopt a throughly professional approach. While insisting on accountability, it (the University) should also ensure a proper academic climate and the necessary autonomy to experiment with new, creative and innovative ideas impinging on the university system as a whole. Such experiments are all the more necessary in the so called 'traditional' disciplines, if they have to safeguard their rightful place and also to avoid the danger of being eased out of the open university system which shows a strong propensity towards remunerative, income generating and self-financing courses and programmes. A proper reorientation of the entire staff would instil the necessary self-confidence in them to play their roles properly at the national and the international levels.

An enlightened academic leadership with a firm grasp of the institutional reality in all its shades and hues should be able to provide the necessary inspiration for the staff to become fully conscious of their own academic potential and that of the system. The distortions and aberations affecting the entire educational system in India have had their fair share in IGNOU too. Nevertheless, IGNOU's youthfulness can absorb the initial shocks and tribulations and yet emerge victorious, provided the negative tendencies are tackled appropriately through proper training and professional guidance. IGNOU's experience during the first decade of its existence has not been very different from that of other institutions in India in certain crucial areas. The difference, however, is to be seen in the magnitude of its potential, the amount of material resources at its disposal the success of its many academic programmes, and the possibility that still exists in the University to fullfill the intended goals which very few institutions in India can boast of. Whether IGNOU can shake off its present lethargy and consolidate some of its valuable gains to create a firm base for distance education in the country is a question which remains to be answered. None can answer this question better than the teachers of IGNOU themselves. But, will they?

References

Gupta, M.L (1986), "Finanaces of Correspondence Education", *Journal of Higher Education*, Vol.2, Nos. 1-3, New Delhi, University Grants Commission.

Indira Gandhi National Open University Act (1985) - IGNOU, New Delhi

IGNOU (1988 -1995), The Annual Reports for the period 1987 - 1994.

IGNOU (1989 - 1996), Vice Chancellor's Reports to the Convocations 1-7, New Delhi.

IGNOU (1996) The Vice-Chancellor's Report to the Seventh Convocation, New Delhi.

IGNOU (1999) The Vice-Chancellor's Report to the Tenth convocation, New Delhi.

Mulay, Vijaya (1986), UGC Report on the State of Correspondence Education in India, New Delhi (Unpublished).

Reddy, Ram G. (1986), *Ivory Towers Thrown Open*, Sterling Publishers, New Delhi.

Reddy, Lakshmi (1995), Consolidated Report of Counselling Feedback Reports of the year 1993. Regional Services Division, IGNOU, New Delhi (Unpblished).

Bibliography

AIU *Handbook* 2001, Association of Indian Universities, New Delhi.

Arger, Geof (1990): "Distance Education in the Third World: Critical Analysis on the Promise and Reality" *Open Learning*, June, 1990

Arger, Geof (1993), *Distance Education in Asia and the Pacific*, Vol.1. UNESCO

Armengol, M.C and Stojanovic, L. (1999) " Distance Education: A Distance Force For Restructuring the Latin American University". File:\\C:/ICDE-papers\35-cases Armengol.htm.

Armengol, M.C and Stojanovic, L. (1999) "Distance Education: A Decision Force for the Latin American University" File://c:\ICDE. Papers/35-Casas Armengol.htm

Basu, Aparna (1991): "Higher Education in Colonial India" in *Higher Education in India: Retrospect and Prospect*, Ed. Moonis Raza, Association of Indian Universities, New Delhi.

Basu, Sisir(1996), "Regular Telecasts by IGNOU: Feedback from Students", *Indian Journal of Open Learning*", Vol.5 No.1 January 1996.

Bates, A.W (1995), "Creating the Future: Developing Vision in Open Learning" in *Open and Distance Learning Today*, Ed. Fred Lockwood, Routledge, London and New York, p.47

Bates, A.W. (1994) "The Growth of Technology in Distance Education" in *The Role of Technology in Distance Education*, Ed. A.W. Bates, Croom Helm, London and Sydney, p.7

Bittar, Ramona Akl (1999), "Latin American Distance Education Universities: Research For the Future", File://c:\ICDE-papers\32-AKL-Bittar.htm

Blom, Dangny (1995), "Cultural and social aspects of new technologies in education: A European perspective: in *One World Many Voices: Quality in Open Learning*, Ed. David Sewart, 17th World Conference of ICDE, selected papers, 1995, Vol.1., pp.18-19

Bridgeman, Neol (1999)," The Global Virtual Univeristy", File://C:\ICDE-Papers/67-Tiffin.htm

Chakraborty, Kashi Nath (1994): "A critical Study of the 1990-1994 Enrolement in the National Open School", *Indian Journal of Open Learning*, Vol.3. No.2 July 1994.

Costello, Neil (1993), "Organisational cultures and distance learning" *Open Learning* ., June 1992.

Danaher, Patric, Leo, Barlet and Leonie, Rowan (1995) "Interrogating constructions of technology by Australian distance educators", *epistolo didaktika* 1995/1, pp.48-69.

Daniel John (1999) "Distance Learning in the Era of Networks: What are the Key Technologies?", *Pan Commonwealth Forum: Empowerment Through Knowledge and Technology, Brunei Darussalam*, 1-5 March 1999.

Daniel, John S (1995): "Preface", in *Open and Distance Learning Today,* Ed. Fred Lockwood, Routledge, London and New York.

DEC-IGNOU (1995) *Open Universities in India – Academic Programmes –* IGNOU 1995.

Deshpande, P.M. (1992) "Yashwantrao Chavan Maharastra Open University", *Indian Journal Of open Learning* (IJOL), Vol.1, No.1, pp.5-10.

Dhanarajan, G. (1996): "Key Note Address" to *National Seminar on Students Support Systems in Distance Education,* IGNOU, New Delhi February 7-8, 1996.

Dhanarajan, G., Swift, D.F. and Hope A. (1994) "Planning for Self-financing at the Open Learning Institute of Hong Kong" in *Economics of Distance Education: Recent Experiences,* Ed. G. Dhanarajan, Hong Kong.

Dunbar, Raden (1991) "Adapting distance education for Indonesians: Problems with learner hetronomy and a strong oral tradition", *Distance Education,* 12(2), 1991.

Government of India (1974) *Working Group Report on National Open University* (Unpublished), New Delhi. (popularly known as the Parthasarathy Committee Report).

Gupta, M.L (1986), "Finanaces of Correspondance Education", *Journal of Higher Education,* Vol.2, Nos. 1-3, New Delhi, University Grants Commission.

Hall, James W (1987), "Bridging the Technology – Pedagogy gap" in *Distance Education and the Mainstream,* Eds. Peter Smith and Mavis Kelly, Croom Helm, London, New York, Sydney pp.44-56

Hawkridge, David (1995). "The Big Bang Theroy in Distance Education" in *Open and Distance learning Today,* Ed. Fred Lockwood, Routledge, London and New York, pp.6.9

Holmberg, Borje (1989): *Theory and Practice of Distance Education,* Routledge, London & NewYork. ICDL(1999) Data Base, IGNOU Library, New Delhi.

Holt and Thompson (1995) "Responding to the technological imperative: the experience of an open and distance education institution", *Distance Education,* Vol.16 No.1, 1995, pp 43-64

IGNOU (1988-995), *The Annual Reports* for the period 1987-1994.

IGNOU (1989-1996), *Vice Chancellor's Report* to the Convocation 1-7, New Delhi.

IGNOU (1995), IGNOU: *A Profile,* New Delhi.

IGNOU (1995),Vice-Chancellor's Report to the Sixth Convocation, New Delhi.

IGNOU (1996), *The Vice-Chancellor's Report to the Seventh Convocation,* New Delhi.

IGNOU (1999), The *Vice-Chancellor's* Report to the Tenth convocation, New Delhi.

Indira Gandhi National Open University Act (1985) - IGNOU, New Delhi

Inquay, S. (1992): "Distance Education in Ethiopia: A Rejoinder", *Distance Education,* 13(2), 1992.

Johnson, Henry C (1995), "Distance Education in Latin America: the Challenge to create a technology of hope" in *One World Many Voices Quality in Open and Distance Learning,* Ed. David Sewart, Vol.1, 17th World Conference for Distance Education, Birmingham, pp.24-27

Jose Chander, N. (1991), *Management of Distance Education*, Sterling publishers, New Delhi

Kirkwood, A .91995)," Over the thresold: Media technologies for home learning" in *Open and Distance Learning Today*, op.cit. pp. 130;134

Kirkwood, Adrian (1995), "Over the threshold: Media Technologies for Home Learning" in *Open and Distance Learning Today*, Ed. Fred Lockwood, Routledge, London and NewYork.

Laser, W. (1995), "Some problems to implement distance education in developing countries", 17th World Conference of ICDE, Selected Papers, Ed. David Sewart, 17th ICDE Conference, Birmingham.

Laser, W. (1995), Commenting on the limited resources and periodical cuts in funding of distance education institutions in the developing countries, says: "As a consequence institutions have to lower their recurrent costs by cutting down teaching staff employed at the central institution, by offering relatively poor tutorial and counselling services and by reducing the quality of learning material. Drop-out rate then increased and the efficiency of the system is considerably affected." W. Lasser (1995), "Some problems to implement distance education in developing countries", 1995, 17th World Conference Papers. ICDE, Vol.1, pp. 303-306.

Ljosa Earling (1991), "Distance Education in Europe and Models for Organising Future Co-operation", ICDE *Bulletin*, Vol. 25, Jan. 1991.

Lomas, Colin, (1999), "The Dangers of Disenfranchising the Disadvantaged through Current Developments of information and Learning Technology (ILT) "or" will the PC replace the teacher or the book?" File://C:/ICDE-Papers\36-Lomascolin.htm.

Manjulika S., and Reddy, V.V. (1996): *Distance Education in India: A Model for Developing Countries*, Vikas publishing House, New Delhi.

Martin, Barbara (1987), "Distance Education in Kenya: A Third World View" in *Distance Education and the Mainstream*, op.cit. pp. 57-73

Miller and Husmann (1995) "Cultural considerations in the offering of courses through Distance Education Technologies", *Indian Journal of Open Learning*, Vol.4 No.1, 1995, pp. 7-10

Miller, Micheal T. (1995): "Cultural Considerations in the offering of Courses through Distance Education Technologies" *Indian Journal of Open Learning*, Vol. 4 No. 1 January 1995.

Moore, Michael G. (1995) "American Distance Education: A Short Literature Review" in *Open and Distance Learning Today* op.cit., pp.32-41

Mulay, Vijaya (1986) *Reports of the Committee on Correspondence Courses*, University Grants Commission (Unpublished).

Mulay, Vijaya (1986), UGC *Report on the State of Correspondance Education in India*, New Delhi (Unpublished).

Mulenga, F.M. (1987): "Distance Education at the University of Zambia" *Open Learning*, November 1987.

Oliveira, J.B.A and Rumble, G (1991) "Distance Education in Latin America: A Review", *Open Learning*, February 1991.

O'Rouke, Jennifer *et al* (1995), *"Distance education in Canada: 1995" 17th World Conference of* ICDE, *selected papers*, 1995, Vol. 1 pp. 28-29

Parer, Michael S. (1994) *Unlocking Open Learning,* Centre for Distance Learning, Monash University, Australia

Perry, Walter (1976) Open University: The Open University Press, Milton Keynes, The United Kingdom.

Perry, Wlter (1987), Open University: A personal Account of the First Vice-Chancellor. The Open University Press, Milton Keynes, The United Kingdom, pp. 22, 213; 215

Peter, Otto (1998) *Learning and Teaching in Distance Education: Analysis and Interpretations from an International Perspective*, Chapter 6, Kogan Page, London.

Prasad, V.S. (1992), "Dr. B.R. Ambedkar Open University: A Decennail Perspective", Indian Journal of Open Learning, Vol.1, No.2, pp.11-18.

Ram Reddy, G. (1986) *Ivory Towers Thrown Open*, Sterling Publishers, New Delhi

Reddy, Lakshmi (1995), *Consolidated Report of Counselling Feedback Reports of the Year 1993*. Regional Services Division, IGNOU, New Delhi (Unpblished).

Renga Ramanujam (1995), *Reflections on Distance Education for India,* Manak Publications, New Delhi, Chapters 2 & 3.

Rumble G (1985): "Distance Education in Latin America: Models for the 80s", *Distance Education*, 6(2).

Russell, Thomas (1992), Bucking the Trend: "Low-Tech Telecommunications", *Indian Journal of Open Learning,* Vol.1 No.1, 1992, pp33-36

Sewart, David (1995), Ed. *One World Many Voices: Quality in Open and Distance Learning* Vol.2, 17th World Conference for Distance Education, Birmingham, See the selection on "Technology"

Sewart, David (1995): Ed. *One World Many Voices: Quality in Open and Distance Learning,* 17th World Conference for Distance Education, Birmingham. 26-30 June 1995.

Singh, B. *et al* (1994) *Correspondence/Distance Education in India: An In depth Study,* Ed. By B.N. Koul, Indira Gandhi National Open University, New Delhi.

Smith, Peter and Mavis, Kelly (1989), Eds. *Distance Education and the Mainstream,* Croom Helm. London. New York. Sydney.

Sparkes, John (1984) "Pedagogic Differences Between Media" in *The Role of Technology in Distance Education*, op.cit., pp. 207-222.

Styler, W.E. (1984): *Adult Education and Political Systems,* Department of Adult Education, University of Nottingham, The United Kingdom.